Smoke Screen

WOMEN'S SMOKING
AND SOCIAL CONTROL

Lorraine Greaves

Fernwood Publishing
Halifax, Canada
Scarlet Press
London, England

Editing: Anne Webb
Design and production: Beverley Rach
Printed and bound in Canada by: Hignell Printing Limited

Published in Canada by:
Fernwood Publishing
Box 9409, Station A
Halifax, Nova Scotia
Canada, B3K 5S3

Published in the rest of the world by:
Scarlet Press
5 Montague Road
London E8 2HN, England

Fernwood Publishing Company Limited gratefully acknowledges the financial support of The Ministry of Canadian Heritage and the Canada/Nova Scotia Cooperation Agreement on Cultural Development.

We are grateful for the permission granted to reprint copyright material in this publication. Every effort was made to obtain permission for the illustrations contained herein.

A catalogue record for this book is available from the British Library.

Scarlet Press
ISBN 1 85727 058 4

Canadian Cataloguing in Publication Data
Greaves, Lorraine

Smoke screen

Includes bibliographical references.
ISBN 1-895686-57-1

1. Women -- Tobacco use -- Canada. 2. Tobacco habit -- Canada.
3. Smoking -- Canada. I. Title.

HV5746.G73 1996   362.29'6'082   C95-950330-7

CONTENTS

to my parents

Rene and Alec Greaves

ACKNOWLEDGEMENTS

This book is the result of several years of research, activism and discussion on the issue of women and tobacco. A constant source of inspiration in my activist efforts is the International Network of Women Against Tobacco (INWAT). In particular, INWAT president, Deborah McLellan has provided me with constant support, ideas and fun. Patti White, Amanda Amos, Vera Luiza da Costa e Silva, Mira Aghi, Judith McKay, Claire Chollat-Traquet, Annie Sasco, Michelle Bloch, Jerie Jordan, Abby Hoffman, and the members of the Women's Working Group at ASH (UK), are all dedicated activists. They and hundreds of other women in INWAT work tirelessly to affect policy, programs and attitudes regarding the situation of women and smoking throughout the world.

Bobbie Jacobson brought discussion of women and tobacco issues to the fore in the 1980s in the United Kingdom and did much to initiate a feminist analysis of women and smoking. She also did much to begin breaking down the sexism in the global movement dedicated to reducing the effects of tobacco. Hilary Graham continues to offer great analysis and insight into many of the issues raised in this book.

In Canada, my long-time allies while working on women and tobacco concerns include the members of the Women and Tobacco Working Group and activists in Canadian women's health movement. Between these groups and many women at Health Canada who have committed themselves to building research, policy and programs concerning women and tobacco, much ground-breaking work has been accomplished.

Over the past eight years, many organizations have given me opportunities to think, speak, learn or do research about women's smoking. Among them are Health Canada, the Canadian Council on Smoking and Health, the National Cancer Institute, the World Health Organization, the International Union Against Cancer, the Department of Sociology and Anthropology at Monash University, the Health Education Authority and the QUIT campaign. I am grateful to all of these.

Special mention goes to Constance Backhouse, a constant source of encouragement; Sandra Kirby, a wonderful colleague and researcher; and Joanne Finkelstein, who offered guidance and critical insight on aspects of this work. Also, thanks to Alex Hartmann for her relentless on-line searches, Barbara Novak, for editorial support and Louise Karch for reading the manuscipt at a crucial point.

My appreciation is extended to both Errol Sharpe of Fernwood Publishing and Avis Lewallen at Scarlet Press, the publishers, for their progressive ideas and enthusiasm for this book. Errol Sharpe and the team at Fernwood offered insights and criticism that has made this a much improved book. Special thanks to the editor, Anne Webb, for her diligence and care; Brenda Conroy, for her work on permissions and promotions, and Beverley Rach, for her creativity and attention to detail. Also, many thanks to Joanne Sinclair for typing and Donna Davis for proofreading.

Most important, though, are the many women who have talked with me over the years about how aspects of smoking affect their lives. Without their insights and analyses, the issues raised in this book would not be as clear.

To all of my family and friends, particularly Lucas, Simon, David, Johanna, John and Margaret, a great thank-you for much assistance and support.

FOREWORD

When I was fifteen, I went on a school trip to see a play. After the play we had some free time. Four of us, all girls, went to a restaurant, pooled our money and bought a package of Belvedere cigarettes. I remember the package was a strong blue, and it was attractive to look at and nice to the touch. We crowded into a booth, ordered soft drinks and I had my first cigarette. It was awful. I immediately felt very dizzy but, after several more attempts at smoking, I learned to like it and smoked cigarettes on and off until I was into my thirties.

My three friends also became smokers. Two became pregnant and had to get married. Two were abused by their boyfriends, and later their husbands. Another was sent to a psychiatric hospital because she had a normal reaction to a stressful life.

I have long been interested in smoking, violence and women's stories. My interest has led me to many places, meetings, women, books and agencies. After I conquered my own addiction, I worked to bring more attention to women, women's stories and smoking in order to give women and smoking the understanding they deserve. In my view, women's smoking is often a response to women's lot. Inequality and oppression, whether in the form of violence or poverty or overwork, are powerful forces, moulding women's behaviour. To understand smoking in this way is to understand more about women.

INTRODUCTION

This book is about women's smoking, identity and social reactions to women's smoking. To truly understand women's smoking it is necessary to ask women what meaning it has for them. This meaning is often complicated by the astute strategies of the tobacco industry, a strong political economy surrounding tobacco and ever changing social norms and regulations regarding smoking.

I believe that women's smoking is socially adaptive and is often implicitly socially approved. In this book, some women smokers offer insights into how smoking helps them adapt to and comply with their life circumstances. Smoking often appears to act as a buffer or screen, between individual, internal, lived experience and external social realities.

A massive global political economy maintains tobacco as a legal drug despite its demonstrated damage and death toll, and women and other groups are being recruited to increase the marketing possibilities globally. This marketing facilitates the continued acceptability of tobacco as a drug of self-medication, a source of identity formation and a form of social control.

In this book, I analyze the cultural and socioeconomic context of women's smoking, primarily in Canada and other industrial countries, but also in Third World countries where smoking by women is increasing.[1] Women's own interpretations of smoking are central to understanding how and why smoking takes root, persists and sustains itself. But such interpretations have typically been overlooked or avoided by both policymakers and health promoters.

Central to understanding these interpretations is the recognition that smoking cigarettes also functions to maintain elements of social and economic life. Women's overconsumption of tobacco, unlike alcohol and drugs, does not interfere with their carrying out their social roles and obligations. Pregnant smokers represent the only exemption to this maxim, explaining the considerable amount of attention given to smoking and pregnancy over the years.

Cigarette smoking is the site of much controversy and pain as well as legal, economic and moral regulation in late twentieth century North America. Smoking is at once a personal act and a social act, with serious medical and economic consequences. Science allows us to understand smoking's effects in more dramatic detail each year, and the toll of smoking on our personal and collective health and economy is becoming better understood.

But women's smoking has generally escaped serious analysis. Long considered secondary to men's smoking, even medical research on the effects of smoking on women has lagged behind. In general, data on women's smoking prevalence are collected in industrial countries, but are much less available for Third World countries. The available information is inconsistent and difficult to compare as no standard methods are used to collect it. It is clear that there are wide variations in smoking rates across countries, between urban and rural women and between various age and ethnic/racial groups. The World Health Organization (Chollat-Traquet 1992, Chapter 1), in response to the lack of comparable data, has suggested improved methods of data gathering on women's smoking to facilitate the urgent action required to curtail or prevent the global female smoking epidemic.

Although there are exceptions, women's smoking tends to become established and peak first in industrial countries, in urban areas and among those with higher formal education. Approximately 30 per cent of women in industrial countries smoke but, within and between countries, there remain vast differences in rates by age, socioeconomic status, region, and ethnic and racial group. In Third World countries, women's smoking is less well documented but ranges between 2 and 10 per cent. The World Health Organization offers some partial comparisons. About 10 per cent of African women, between 10 and 40 per cent of Latin American women, about 5 per cent of South East Asian women, 8 per cent of Eastern Mediterranean women and less than 10 per cent of Western Pacific women smoke. However, there are, again, vast variations between regions and subgroups of women. Sometimes women's smoking is culturally prohibited, while chewing or other more traditional modes of tobacco use are more approved. In all countries, negative attitudes toward women's and girls' smoking can distort attempts to collect accurate data. Sociological and cultural analyses of women's smoking are only now being made.

In my view, women experience the world as a series of gendered social and economic circumstances, and smoking must be understood in this context. However, since women occupy some very different locations across such categories as class, race, age and sexual orientation, it is not assumed in this inquiry that all women do or will have a unitary common experience. Therefore, listening to women's own interpretations of smoking is crucial to understanding the complex contradictions involved in initiating and maintaining smoking in an era of increasing regulation and awareness of its negative effects.

Explaining women's smoking cannot be limited to a singular theme. It is not solely a result of targeted advertising campaigns promising freedom or a correlate of women's liberation, both of which are often proffered as explanations. Some tobacco control or health promotion workers hold these views, revealing a rather ironic uncritical absorption of the industry's famous message, "You've come a long way baby". If this is the cause of smoking, then anyone interested in the status of women would see the cure as more worrisome.

But more seriously, this equation makes women seem passive. It is too simple to assume that women who smoke are pathetically duped by smoking culture, stupidly anti-health or servants of tobacco ads. Women smokers may be passive recipients of external influences, active resisters to aspects of society, or both from time to time. Even as overall smoking declines in Canada, young girls' smoking is surpassing boys' smoking for the first time in history. Trends such as this raise questions that must acknowledge women's agency.

However, the complex and ambivalent views on women's smoking that have emerged over the centuries tend to be embedded in the Western collective consciousness for feminists and non-feminists alike. These ambivalences continue to infect not just the explanations for women's smoking, but also the suggestions for ending it. These contradictions are also embedded in the testimony of women smokers regarding their smoking patterns.

Much of the work being done to solve the problem of women's smoking is undertaken in isolation from women smokers themselves. This is often protective, as it allows advocates and policymakers to create policy and programing according to their own agenda, exempt from the realities of smokers' lives and thoughts and from unintended consequences. This inquiry attempts to break through that divide by offering some insights from women smokers discussed in the context of the history, culture, costs, benefits and values associated with smoking. These must be the key elements in planning future actions on women and smoking.

This book is dedicated to increasing the general understanding of women, as well as smoking, and to uncovering insights that will enhance the future health and welfare of women. It is also intended to inform a collective response to women's smoking. While this inquiry is focused mainly on particular women smokers in industrial countries, and is far from generalizable, I hope that its conclusions will have a deterrent effect on the current globalization of the women's smoking epidemic.

NOTE

1. The term "industrial" is preferred here over other options, such as developed or First World, as it is more descriptive and less evaluative than the latter two. The South/North division does not work here as Australia is often grouped with

Western Europe and North America in this text. "Industrial" is too broad a classification to be used accurately but is relatively benign. I am using the term Third World to refer to the countries in Latin American, Africa, Asia and the Caribbean. While this term, like those used in its place, is controversial, it can be argued that it recognizes the "hierarchical cultural and economic relationship between 'first' and 'third' world countries; it intentionally foregrounds a history of colonization and contemporary relationships of structural dominance between first and third world peoples" (Mohanty, Chandra Talpade; Ann Russo and Lourdes Torres (eds.). *Third World Women and the Politics of Feminism.* Bloomington: Indiana University Press, 1991:x).

Chapter One

INFLUENCES

Historical and Cultural Influences
on Women's Smoking in Industrial Countries

> Women's smoking, like most of women's activities, has always been commented upon. Cultural changes, social pressures, laws and attitudes have influenced women's smoking practices for centuries.

Smoking has had a history fraught with conflict, right from its introduction into Europe by explorers importing it from North America. Tobacco smoking evoked intense reactions and considerable moral and legal regulation. During the 1500s "tobacco-houses" were established for smokers in Europe and pharmacies sold tobacco on prescription only (Corti 1931, Chapters 5 and 6). It is ironic that almost five centuries later in North America, smokers are once again limited to marginal social locations.

In sixteenth century Europe, smoking was described variously as morally depraved, corrupt, a sign of "Indian Barbarianism" and a cure for cancer, asthma, headache, worms and the "diseases of women" (Corti 1931, 58, 75, 79). Since the advent of tobacco use in Europe, women's smoking has been a contentious issue. The invention of manufactured cigarettes in the late 1800s forced the question of women's smoking, just as it caused men's smoking to become both more widespread and a public issue. Prior to this, tobacco had been smoked mainly in pipes and cigars, and had been restricted to men and some working–class women, at least in the European context. Arguments against women's tobacco use centred on it being unfeminine, but the idea that women should have an equal right to smoke grew over the course of two centuries and took a firm hold in industrial countries, especially Canada and the United States, by the early 1900s.

The origins of smoking are unclear. It may have first been established in the Americas among First Nations peoples and spread from there, or it may have arisen independently in Asia (Robicsek 1978). Either way, early tobacco use was considerably different and did not present the health problem that smoking gives rise to today. Among First Nations peoples, tobacco had, and has, a sacred and medicinal use. Tobacco is used as an offering to the spirit world to give thanks to the Creator, protect travellers, console the bereaved, welcome guests, induce peace or prayer, cure illness and establish bonds. There is no evidence that these practices led to habituation or were even recreational (Columbia School of Social Work 1992). Indeed, only relatively recently has the conversion to smoking cigarettes become a serious health issue among First Nations peoples.

RESISTANCE TO TOBACCO

> Why is it that among the female sex the women who lead blameless, regular lives are the least frequently addicted to smoking? (Tolstoi 1891, 179)

By the 1800s the opposition to tobacco use, and specifically to cigarettes, had grown to include several organized groups. Several women's groups, some feminist, were key in the anti- tobacco movement around the turn of the century in North America. Many women temperance leaders believed that tobacco corrupted men and led them away from their responsibilities to women. In Canada, the Women's Christian Temperance Union (WCTU) named the problem the "Cigarette Evil," and it briefly claimed attention equal in intensity to that of their fights against alcohol and opiate use. Opposition to cigarette smoking, sales to minors, opium trading and narcotics use was worked into the educational goals, pledges and activities of the organization. Its energy and commitment to these issues had a short-lived but profound effect on the development of legislation and public policy in Canada in the early years of this century. This culminated in the (unsuccessful) push for Canadian legislation in 1903 which sought a total ban on cigarette importation and manufacture.

By 1909 the WCTU had been consulted by cabinet, had had bills submitted to it for approval, and was attributed the power to "turn out a Government." It credited itself with "frightening" the Tobacco Trust into spending $20,000 to defeat an anti-cigarette campaign (McKee 1927, 82).

In the United States, women such as Lucy Page Gaston, a Chicago educator who organized the Chicago Anti-Cigarette League in 1899 and the National Anti-Cigarette League in 1901, were in the forefront of the anti-tobacco movement (Troyer and Markle 1983, 30). By 1911, the Anti-Cigarette League of America (now renamed to include Canadian branches) and the Non-Smokers' Protective League of America were formed. The concerns of these groups were almost identical to those of the contemporary non-smokers' rights associations; they advocated restricting sales to minors, smoke-free transport and the right to clean air.

These anti-cigarette forces became aligned with some business leaders, such as Henry Ford, and came to view smoking as a deterrent to worker productivity. Together, they were successful in achieving partial tobacco prohibition and numerous other legislative controls in the United States. They argued, without evidence, that tobacco use was harmful to health, morally degenerate and led to the use of other drugs (Troyer and Markle 1983, 38). A final argument in the anti-cigarette movement of this period was for the right of non-smokers to clean air. In the USA, in 1901, twelve states passed laws prohibiting the sale of tobacco; however, all these laws were repealed by 1927 (Corti 1931, 266).

Despite the general focus on men's and boys' cigarette use, women were also targeted in the publicity of the anti-tobacco movement, often in posters and educational campaigning:

> There was a time when at every street corner in the United States was a poster depicting a mother with a baby in her arms and a cigarette in her mouth; there were no words—the mere presentment, it was hoped, would have a deterrent effect. (Corti 1931, 266)

The momentum of the battle against tobacco was lost in both Canada and the United States by the end of the First World War. In 1919, the wcTU felt forced to concentrate on the (alcohol) Prohibition question. According to McKee:

> Little did we know what a body blow the war would give to the struggling reform! It fairly asphyxiated the public conscience, where tobacco was concerned, and it levelled the one-time barrier between the cigarette and women. (McKee 1927, 98)

In addition, key feminists, such as Nellie McClung, eventually left the temperance movement to pursue more diversified political goals such as women's suffrage and general female emancipation. The loosening of the social mores of the 1920s further contributed to the diminished strength of the woman-based anti-tobacco movement. At the same time, the availability and advertising of manufactured cigarettes, which were promoted as more "ladylike" than cigars or pipes, set the stage for women's increased consumption.

The end of this important era in women's organized responses to the cigarette issue coincided with the beginning of significant levels of consumption of cigarettes by women. In the industrial countries, over the next several decades it became increasingly acceptable for women to smoke cigarettes.

FOCUSING ON WOMEN
The first cigarette advertisements explicitly directed at women in North America, the United Kingdom and other industrial countries appeared in the

late 1920s. In conjunction with other social changes, this deliberate targeting of the female market effectively launched the widespread use of cigarettes by women in these countries. The social acceptability of women's smoking continued to increase during the 1930s and by the end of the Second World War had gained wide acceptance.

During the Second World War, women were required to enter the paid labour force to replace male labour while men were in the forces. This shift in roles proved women's strength and adaptability to varied types of work. Prejudices about women's place and role were temporarily suspended and previously "masculine" behaviours, such as smoking, were more easily adopted by women.

At this point, it served the interests of industry and patriotism to have women take on the roles of men. For the tobacco companies, a large, untapped market of women awaited its advertising and product development. Tobacco companies were also patriotic supporters of the men in the services, and often ran advertising campaigns exhorting those at home to show their support for the soldiers by sending them cartons of cigarettes. Prior to the first articles in the 1940s that directly linked health problems and smoking, and prior to widespread medical research into smoking, tobacco advertising directly appealing to women increased (Ernster 1985; Howe 1984, 4).

Not until 1950 did any organized lobbying against tobacco by health groups begin again in the US, Canada and UK. At first it was believed that smoking- related diseases were male-specific, but the increased exposure of women to long-term tobacco use revealed smoking-related morbidity and mortality in females as well. Even so, prior to the 1980s, the major focus of the medical research on smoking-related diseases was male smokers.

FROM IMMORALITY TO FREEDOM
Manufactured cigarettes have been available for little more than a century. From the late 1800s to the 1920s, smoking by women was associated with the rebellious and the marginal, and was the occupational symbol of prostitution (Banner 1983, 76). The number of women using cigarettes has been significant in industrial countries only since the Second World War.

While the anti-tobacco crusaders of this century concern themselves with both health and environmental issues, their principal concern in the early decades was the drift away from virtue that smoking represented. Women smokers were fallen women; they were "sluts," "whores" and "sinners." So well entrenched was this equation that smoking in public was a brazen act. As early as 1908, a woman in New York was arrested for smoking a cigarette (Cook and Milner 1991, 12).

Despite the hint of freedom occasioned by women's experiences during the First World War, the 1920s brought a return to the image of women as domestic and maternal (Ehrenreich and English 1979, Chapter 5). Homemakers and mothers did not smoke. The apparent conflict between increasing freedom for women and the anti-cigarette lobby was exploited with steadfast resolve by the marketers of cigarettes. Beginning in the 1920s, the Great American Tobacco Company made a concerted effort to erase the taboo against women smoking in public. Feminism was used as a marketing ploy and entered the "jargon of consumerism" (Ewen 1976, 160).

A.A. Brill, hired by the company to consult on strategy, was unequivocal:

> Some women regard cigarettes as symbols of freedom .... Smoking is a sublimation of oral eroticism; holding a cigarette in the mouth excites the oral zone. It is perfectly normal for women to want to smoke cigarettes. Further, the first women who smoked probably had an excess of masculine components and adopted the habit as a masculine act. But today the emancipation of women has suppressed many of the feminine desires. More women now do the same work as men do .... Cigarettes, which are equated with men, become **torches of freedom**. (Ewen 1976, 160; emphasis in original)

As a result, the 1929 Easter parade in New York City included a company-organized and much publicized group of cigarette smoking women, lighting "torches of freedom" as a protest against women's inequality.

This marketing coup was accomplished with the co-operation of leading feminists in the United States. Ewen calls this "commercialized feminism" and, while not limited to tobacco, its derivatives remain a dominant approach in cigarette marketing in the 1990s.

Lacking evidence confirming the effects of smoking on health, the opponents of tobacco in the 1920s had little to work with other than hygiene and morality arguments. It was easy to perceive anti-cigarette lobbying as anti-woman, anti-feminist and anti-choice. From being a badge of prostitution prior to the First World War, cigarette smoking in the 1920s became a symbol of women's freedom in the dominant culture and a challenge to Victorian mores. Smoking became firmly aligned with dress reform, bobbed hair, nightclubbing and suffrage.

It took six decades for this link between smoking and women's freedom to be explicitly countered by health and social commentators. The strength of tobacco's addictive qualities only gradually became clear as smokers became aware of the difficulty of quitting. Even so, the more profound "loss of freedom" attached to smoking cigarettes was (and is) a difficult concept to transmit in light of the continued use of the freedom motif in tobacco advertising.

Hannah, July 1934

MASCULINE TO FEMININE

The *masculinity* implied by smoking was a key part of the cultural symbolism challenged by women smokers during the 1920s in industrial countries. Smoking tobacco had almost always been a man's domain, particularly due to the preponderance of pipe and cigar smoking prior to the advent of the manufactured cigarette.[1] If equality was understood as being "equal to" men, then it followed that women should be allowed to do whatever men could. Smoking cigarettes for women clearly fit in this domain.

In her analysis of the cultural meaning of cross-dressing in the West, Marjorie Garber discusses the role of smoking in blurring gender lines. She notes that in the early decades of the twentieth century, smoking was generally acknowledged as a "male" taste, and lesbians in particular were seen to have an affinity for smoking as part of their adoption of male attire and attitude. Women such as Romaine Brooks, Una Troubridge, Radclyffe Hall and Colette were illustrative of this connection between "social and sexual liberation" (Garber 1992, 156). "Liberation" was understood by the dominant culture to mean the ability and opportunity to act (and smoke) like men.

By the 1930s, an increasingly unisex trend emerged in this culture which included cigarettes as an item of consumption for women and matched the lessening of differences between male and female dress (Ernster 1985, 337). Since then, along with the development of more sophisticated definitions of sexual equality, there have been six decades of elastic cultural definitions of women's smoking. Even so, the link between smoking and representations of maleness remains in some tobacco advertising and in popular culture. Garber sees this as clearly illustrated in movies featuring a gender blurring component. *Victor/Victoria* and *Boy, What a Girl!* are two such movies where smoking a cigar is critical to the gender twists in the plot (Garber 1992, 156).

(Hetero)Sexuality

By the 1940s and 1950s, cigarettes became a crucial erotic prop and a way of increasing one's attractiveness to men. This shift from masculine representations not only allowed the marketers of tobacco to access the large heterosexual women's market, but it reinforced the North American cultural links between smoking, power and sexual challenge.

Garber analyses this shift from associating women's smoking with lesbianism to portraying it as a glamourizing activity of heterosexual women. She suggests it is really a way of obfuscating questions of sexual orientation and shifting the focus to questions of class (Garber 1992, 157). Indeed, from the forties until the eighties, tobacco marketers concentrated on associating cigarettes with classy sophistication.

A contemporary example of promoting (and exploiting) heterosexuality was the (thwarted) R.J. Reynolds' Dakota campaign in 1990. This campaign was premised on targeting the "virile" female in her twenties who liked to do what her boyfriend was doing. This was an attempt to secure the blue-collar women's market and was one of many segmented marketing strategies of the tobacco companies that emerged as the overall North American market shrank. Some of these were directed at elite young women, such as the campaigns launched through fashion magazines that include images of women smoking on the runways of fashion shows (Amos 1990b).

Such marketing strategies clearly reflect the values of patriarchy and capitalism in that they support the institution of heterosexuality and enhance profits. It was strategic and profitable several decades ago for the tobacco companies to override any lingering association of women's smoking with lesbianism (or even "mannishness"), just as it was strategic and profitable in the 1920s to override the association with prostitution.

On a more fundamental level, the contemporary marketing strategies also reinforce patriarchal and capitalist definitions of heterosexual women's smoking through brand development and the use of the media to display appropriate imagery and cultural symbolism. Thus, smoking has become part of the "cultural propaganda of heterosexuality" described by Adrienne Rich in her critical essay on "compulsory heterosexuality" (Rich 1980, 660). More recently, brand development and advertising of tobacco in the US has focused on blacks, Latinos, and gay and lesbian populations.

Over this century, then, in industrial countries the cultural meaning of women's smoking as it relates to gender relations has moved from a symbol of being *bought* by men (prostitute), to being *like* men (lesbian/mannish/androgynous), to being *able to attract* men (glamourous/heterosexual). Sexual liberals may argue that this reflects historical differences in the power and control of a woman over her sexual existence.

However, some sexual radicals would see this as evidence of further entrenchment of the institution of heterosexuality, an erasure of sexual orientation issues and a manipulation of the concept of women's power. The tobacco companies cover all this ground by simultaneously appealing to both the equality-seeking, freedom-loving, challenging woman ("You've come a long way, baby" of Virginia Slims), as well as to the heterosexually defined, male-identified woman (the virile female of the Dakota campaign).

CAPITALISM AND UPWARD MOBILITY

The elasticity of the cultural meaning of women's smoking has reflected the needs of capitalism through the decades of this century. By the 1930s, the marketing of cigarettes to Western women was accomplished by increasingly direct targeting in advertising and product development. Testimonial advertising in women's magazines began and the links between smoking and beauty, slimness, athleticism and sexuality were established. In addition, approximately 30 per cent of the female Hollywood-based film heroines in the 1930s smoked, compared to only 2.5 per cent of female villains (Ernster 1985, 337). In this decade, young, urban (American) women took up smoking which resulted in a doubling of demand over that of 1920.

The 1930s were the pivotal decade for establishing the interpretation of women's smoking as both "good" and culturally superior, particularly in North America. Elegance and sophistication were the marketing keys in a decade of economic depression. The cigarette could be a small, conspicuous symbol of pleasure, leisure and gentility in a mass consumer culture which had an interest in eroding class divisions and enhancing social bonds (Ewen 1976, 89, 95). The presentation of the cigarette as a sophisticated, genteel product and an affordable symbol of upward mobility fulfilled these goals well. During a decade of class conflict and tension, the cigarette was one small equalizer; smoking provided an image of pleasure and consumption which was promoted in cinema, magazines and radio.

In 1939, the American *Life* magazine featured a photo essay of a Philip Morris sponsored lecture tour giving women lessons in cigarette smoking. The etiquette of women's smoking was defined, including the proper ways to open packages and light, smoke, hold and extinguish cigarettes. This strategy not only built up the market of women smokers, but it actively pursued audiences of "clubwomen," nurses and charm-school graduates (Life 1986, 87–88). Even Emily Post offered guidelines for "well-bred" smokers in *Good Housekeeping* (1940, 37). She makes it clear that women should not smoke on the street and definitely not while wearing a bridal veil!

Using strategies such as this, the tobacco companies constructed women's smoking as a subject of "etiquette," infused it with a white, bourgeois sensibility, and re-created it as heterosexually acceptable and attractive.

PATRIOTISM AND WAR

The androgynous portrayal of smoking reappeared in Europe and North America with the Second World War as women were once again drawn into the labour force, often to do non-traditional (male) work. The links between cigarettes and patriotism, established during the First World War, were more fully developed during the Second World War. Women were featured in non-traditional work roles (with cigarettes present in the images) and in active service roles as well (Jacobson 1986, 44). In addition, in both the United Kingdom and the United States, cigarettes were declared as essential as food and were rationed in a similar manner. In 1941, Roosevelt declared tobacco an essential crop and even relieved US tobacco farmers of military service.

Thus, the links between smoking, equality, masculinity and patriotism were strengthened in these Western countries and overshadowed remaining moral objections to women smoking cigarettes. The manufacturers of tobacco again made sure to

"I STARTED SMOKING CAMELS FOURTEEN YEARS AGO____"

MRS. ADRIAN ISELIN, II

CAMELS ARE MADE FROM FINER, MORE EXPENSIVE TOBACCOS THAN ANY OTHER POPULAR BRAND

Camel's costlier tobaccos are Milde

connect the comfort of the "boys" abroad with the availability of cigarettes, a practice begun during the First World War. In Canada, newspapers listed the names of donors to the tobacco fund with the amount of their donations. One such campaign, run by the Overseas League Tobacco and Hamper Fund, solicited donations to keep the "boys and girls overseas, including prisoners of war, well-supplied" (*The Star Weekly*, 25 November 1944). In the same paper, the C.C. MacDonald Tobacco Company advertised for members of the public to "Send the Boys the Best" by remitting three dollars for nine hundred cigarettes to be sent to members of the Canadian Active Services. Patriotism and support for the troops was thereby linked to the purchase of cigarettes, potentially even by non-smokers.[2]

Immediately after the Second World War when large numbers of women were being ushered back into traditional roles, cigarette advertisers introduced a different set of images. Women—usually young, white and middle-class—were represented as wives and lovers expecting reunions or as brides taking cartons of cigarettes on their honeymoons (Ernster 1985, 337). During the 1940s, smoking was increasingly promoted as a companionable leisure activity to be shared by men and women, a theme still dominant in current cigarette promotions.

WORK AND LEISURE

Between 1950 and 1970, the advertisements less frequently showed women as workers, housewives or mothers. Prevailing values instead encouraged middle-class domesticity. Possibly the emerging evidence about the health costs of smoking forced the advertisers to move away from picturing women in active poses, and toward more social and decorative representations of women's smoking. The portrayal of smoking as a leisure activity to be enjoyed in group situations became a more frequent theme of cigarette advertisements featuring women (Sexton and Haberman 1974, 44). Even so, the women featured in cigarette ads were rarely shown with cigarettes in

It's not just a cigarette.
It's a few minutes of your own.

you are here.

Made with gently steamed
tobacco for a uniquely rich taste.

their mouths; most often they were pictured completely disconnected from
the cigarette or the act of smoking. The exception to this pattern was imagery
of men helping women light cigarettes (ibid., 45).

Women's smoking has become increasingly defined by marketers as a
leisure activity and a source of relaxation. In the last two decades, as
women's labour force participation has increased significantly, women
have been viewed by those in advertising as suffering stress and needing
relaxation aids. Cigarettes have been promoted as such aids and tobacco
trade journals have particularly targeted stressed women in the labour force
as an "untapped market" in the West (Jacobson 1986, 48).

The marketers of cigarettes have managed to promote the idea that
women are overstressed workers without picturing them in their work roles.

Only during the 1930s and 1940s were women portrayed in occupational roles in cigarette advertisements, as the marketers created the image of smoking as a mark of independence and action in women. More recently, women have been shown as "deserving" (needing) the pleasure, leisure, satisfaction and self-indulgence represented by smoking their own cigarette, their own way, on their own time.

This marketing approach carries a more complex cultural message: it appears to promote women's independence while it subtly fosters and features women's dependence. The contradiction is artfully contained in the promotion of cigarettes as a prop through which to achieve equality or as a social symbol of pleasure and reward rather than addiction.

Contributing to this pattern, some analysts have superficially correlated the recent increase in smoking among women with the experience of and desire for increased equality felt by many women in the West and elsewhere. Howe, for example, suggests that young women in the US may see cigarette smoking as signifying equality with males, and implies that this will attract them to the habit (1984, 8).

This idea has been nurtured by the effective Virginia Slims campaign slogan; "You've come a long way, baby" features strides in women's equality as a basis for selling women cigarettes. Even health workers, analysts and researchers promoting non-smoking have generally uncritically absorbed this linking of women's liberation with increased smoking, a linkage which allows the continued emphasis in prevention, cessation and research activity to be on individual women's smoking behaviours, including their "choice" to smoke. Comparatively little attention has been paid to the social structural features that foster the patterns of women's attraction and attachment to cigarette smoking in contemporary Western culture.

This interpretation of equality, used to explain and justify women's increasing smoking rates in the 1920s and 1930s, seems rather simplistic in the 1990s when much more is known about the effects of smoking and when women's (and girls') occupational and social identities are considerably more complicated.

GIRLS AND IDENTITY

Today's generation of adolescent girls in industrial countries is in a unique position. It is the first cohort of girls to have been explicitly encouraged by mainstream society to perceive themselves as self-supporting in their future and to have achievement orientations designed to make them economically successful. At the same time, these girls soon come to recognize that fundamental social, economic, "race" and ability inequalities still exist for women and between women. Between the sexes there is still, for example, a persistent wage gap, unequal division of household labour, unequal and insufficient child care options and violence against women. These girls (and boys) who are not members of the dominant culture in this part of the world face further forms of inequality. It is perhaps not surprising that girls' smoking rates are for the first time surpassing boys' in several industrial countries, as girls struggle with considerable dissonance and increasing stress in resolving their identities.

Gilligan, Lyons and Hanmer have studied the transition that elite adolescent girls make in resolving their identity. They note that, at early adolescence, young girls shift from "resisting" and being verbally direct to a more acquiescent and somewhat deflated way of being in the world (Gilligan et al. 1990, 24–25). According to Gilligan et al., the resolve that young girls show in childhood begins to diminish at age twelve as they realize the limitations placed upon them in the world and observe how adult women function within those limitations.

It is around this crucial age when they may try smoking for the first time. As the assertiveness, strength and clarity of early childhood is replaced by confusion, self-doubt and suppression of thought and speech, female adolescence becomes a period of negativity, curtailment of expectations and stress.

The contradictions of female identity emerge with respect to smoking behaviour later in life as well. Elkind's study of the social definition of women's smoking behaviour in Britain involved questioning young adult women, both smokers and non-smokers, about their attitudes toward the symbolic meaning of women's smoking. The non-smokers felt that women's smoking was unladylike or "male" while the smokers were more likely to view it as "liberated." What was most telling was that the smokers saw non-smoking women as having no distinctive identity (Elkind 1985, 1275).

Smokers and non-smokers had divergent, but class-related, views about women's smoking. More working-class women smokers perceived smoking as liberated (and positive) than middle-class women. The working-class women who did not smoke were more likely to perceive non-smoking women as "feminine," while the middle-class non-smokers perceived non-smoking women as "intelligent." While there was more agreement across the two groups on the assessment of smoking among women as "unladylike," the word "liberated" was chosen significantly more often by the working-class women than the middle-class women (ibid.).

CIGARETTES ARE EVERYTHING: THE DIVERSIFICATION OF MESSAGES

There are many contradictions and oppositional themes promoted in the contemporary marketing of tobacco aimed at women. Ironically, cigarettes are often advertised in the context of youthfulness, activity, athleticism and health while their consumption leads to the erosion of precisely these qualities. These messages and images have emerged and re-emerged to match culturally desired images of woman at any given time; it is a manipulative process that has created and supported several changes in the social definition of women's role in industrial countries over the past eight decades. These days the messages target every possible audience in strategic and relevant forms. Unfortunately, the tobacco companies react to the diversity of contemporary women far more comprehensively than do health promotion agencies.

A recent analysis of tobacco advertising appearing in selected Canadian and US women's magazines indicates that many themes are used in contemporary advertising aimed at the women's market (Greaves 1995b). Advertisements promising excitement and freedom predominate with ads representing vitality, freshness and sociability occurring with the next greatest frequency. In addition, there is a significant subset of tobacco advertising reflecting "thin," "light" and "slim" cigarettes, pushing the image of "thin smoke" (typified by Virginia Slims Lights) that clearly implies that cigarettes will assist with weight control.

Despite the tobacco advertising ban begun in 1989 in Canada, tobacco companies are permitted to advertise their sponsorship activities in Canadian magazines, and do so. The ban was overturned in 1995 on the grounds that it contravened freedom of speech provisions in the Charter of Rights. However, tobacco companies have not immediately moved to use this reversal. Many Canadian women also read imported magazines containing significant amounts of tobacco advertising.[3] Its predominance and the revenue magazines receive are calculated by the advertisers to eliminate serious editorial treatment of smoking and health issues from the pages of women's magazines. This strategy has serious implications as women's magazines are a key source of health information for women readers (Amos 1984; ASH 1990).

Other media also contribute to the cultural representations of women's smoking. Films, in particular, have played a key role in attaching meanings to women's smoking over the decades. European and North American movies have been pivotal in glamourizing smoking for heterosexual women and associating women's smoking with erotic sophistication and power. In the 1981 movie *Superman II*, Lois Lane, the heroine, was created as a Marlboro Woman and the backdrop in a crucial scene was a bank of Marlboro vans (Jacobson 1986, 80–81; Magnus 1985). My recent research on the images of smoking and women in contemporary popular media, undertaken for Health Canada, reveals that movies remain a key source of such imagery. For example, in the 1991 Hollywood film, *Basic Instinct*, the main female character uses smoking as a key expression of her personal power (Greaves 1995b).

In my analysis of the "most watched" contemporary films of the past five years in Canada, I have found significant representations of smoking in mainstream film. Approximately every twenty minutes, on average, an image of smoking appears. While the majority represent male smoking, this smoking imagery appears most frequently in films directed at children and youth audiences (Greaves 1995b)[4].

That smoking imagery is directed at young people, in films dominated by questionable female roles, in an industry dominated by men and male-oriented scripts, suggests that film is another key element in the tobacco industry's marketing strategy. There is increasing evidence that tobacco companies pay to have their products represented in films, and there are several examples of direct representation of logos and packages. However, I conclude that the mere representation of smoking, especially in relatively complicated presentations, has far more impact in shoring up smokers' resolve or attracting young people to smoking.

In an era in the West of increased smoking regulations and health knowledge regarding smoking, Sharon Stone's performance in *Basic Instinct*, where she defiantly and successfully continues to smoke in the face of police authority and while under suspicion for murder, stands out as a 1990s testimonial for smoking in the face of oppressive regulations. Having a woman present this message adds power and complexity to the role of women smokers in contemporary times.

Women's smoking patterns in the Third World may be affected by some of these same Western media messages in advertising and film as the cultural and geographical diffusion of women's smoking progresses. The contradictions promoted by tobacco marketing directed toward women linger in the public consciousness internationally. How these images are interpreted is greatly affected by the age and class of their audience. While not the only source of cultural definitions of women's smoking, the advertisers and promoters in concert with various media have played a crucial role in inseminating the Western public mind with powerful conceptions of women's smoking.

HISTORY REPEATS ITSELF

The tobacco industry is illustrative of what Ewen labels "the triumph of capitalism in the twentieth century [in its] ability to define and contend with the conditions of the social realm" (1976, 219). In this sense, from the perspective of analysts and perhaps the tobacco industry as well, cigarettes have become items which serve to limit social change and contain "fantasies of liberation" (ibid.). Consumers of cigarettes may use them as singular events of liberation but eventually experience them as a blanket of suppression and restriction. However, when loaded with symbolism and linked to cultural aspirations by the corporate culture, cigarettes are particularly tantalizing for consumers whose roles are unclear, unequal or unrewarded. Girls, women, minorities and vast populations in the Third World are therefore key groups targeted to enlarge the consumer market for tobacco.

Capitalism's recent advance on several Eastern Bloc countries offers a current example of this process. According to Connolly (1992, 1), Latin

America was the transnational tobacco companies' (TTC) target in the 1960s, and the newly developed nations of Asia were the target during the 1980s. Today, the tobacco giants are pushing into Eastern Europe, China and Africa. In Eastern Europe and the Russian Republic, for example, both R.J. Reynolds and Philip Morris have manufacturing agreements in several countries. Consumers in these countries are faced with new, ubiquitous and

unregulated tobacco advertising, where cigarettes take on cultural meaning in newly capitalist countries. According to Gorecka (1994, 2), women are the key targeted consumer group in Poland and other countries in Eastern Europe and are exposed to massive woman-focused advertising. The result in Poland over the past five years has been an increase in smoking among "blue-collar" women workers, while the higher educated women decreased their smoking.

Similar investments in Asia and Africa have occurred over the past few years. American or European brand cigarettes are a status symbol in many countries. The advantages of marketing to Third World countries are enormous. Faster population growth, less regulation and lower health knowledge create fertile conditions for marketing tobacco. The massive population size in countries like China, whose population already smokes 30 per cent of the world's total cigarette production, and the extremely low female smoking rate in that country (approximately 7 per cent, compared to 60 per cent among men) (Chollat-Traquet 1992, 12) offer possibilities for growth that make North American and European markets pale in comparison. The implications of targeting the Chinese women's market alone are staggering in terms of potential revenue.

There are six main transnational tobacco companies which produce the majority of the world's cigarettes. These six companies are gradually acquiring increased control by systematically buying state controlled tobacco companies and infiltrating the huge markets of the Third World. Typically, several approaches are used to gain control of new markets, including the sale of contraband cigarettes, support of local politicians, transfers of the manufacturing and financial investments to local companies and massive advertising campaigns (Connolly 1992, 3). When US trade threats are added to this set of circumstances, governments are encouraged to legalize foreign brands and welcome TTC investments, thereby opening up lucrative, previously closed markets.

This oligopoly is enhanced by a long historical commitment to tobacco growing and marketing by some governments, particularly in the United States. This commitment produces ambiguous policy and legislative results, and creates a climate for continued growth and complicity between governments and industry. To counter the impact of reduced markets and increased regulation in industrial countries, the tobacco companies have diversified into many other products and markets. In tobacco advertising directed at racial minorities and Third World countries, the transnationals add on what Chapman (1990, 79) labels "white supremacist racism" by linking prosperity, leisure and prestige to the imagery associated with smoking.

Transnational companies will continue to develop markets in economies with few regulations and little legislation controlling the buying and selling of cigarettes. In some countries there are no controls on sales to minors, smoke-free transport or public space and little regulation of the contents of cigarettes. And as there are already more smokers in China alone than in the whole population of the United States, such investments will secure the long term health of the global tobacco industry.

CONCLUSION

Women's cigarette smoking has had a short history in North America. Men's smoking rates are declining faster than women's rates. While women's overall rates are on the decline in several industrial countries, young women's smoking rates are increasing (Amos 1990a). They now surpass young men's rates in Canada, France, Australia, Wales, Scotland, Denmark, Iceland, Norway, England, Sweden, Switzerland and Austria, among other industrial countries. This trend has no historical precedent. Additionally, the low rates of women's smoking in the Third World are just beginning to rise (Chollet-Traquet 1992). Typically, smoking diffuses through populations, establishing itself first among elite men, and working down class and status hierarchies and through the population. Even so, men usually smoke more than women and that relationship remained constant in the industrial world until the mid 1980s. These current trends may eventually lead to the reversal of the traditional gender difference in smoking rates. Globally, the epidemic of women's smoking has only just begun. This pattern is particularly mystifying in light of extensive health knowledge about the risks of smoking.

Explaining these trends is a challenge for health promotion agencies, women's organizations and governments. It is possible that the overall smoking rates for women will continue to decline and the epidemic of women smokers will abate similar to, but later than, the pattern of the male epidemic. Or is there something different about female smokers that is yet to be fully understood? Why has traditional health promotion policy and programing not had the desired effect on women and girls? Are the powerful social and cultural forces affecting women's smoking continuing to do their work? All of these are possibilities.

NOTES

1. Only cigars were allowed in boardrooms and corporate libraries, banks and offices, even after young men began smoking cigarettes around the turn of the century in the US (Banner 1983, 241). By 1929, an advertisement for Edgeworth Pipe Tobacco showed not only maleness associated with pipe smoking, but also wisdom, upward mobility, security and thoughtfulness: "The Boss? . . . . there with the pipe. Men at the top are apt to be pipe-smokers. . . . His pipe helps a man think straight. A pipe is back of most big ideas." (*Saturday Evening Post*, 7 December 1929, quoted in Ewen 1976, 154-55).
2. In 1991, during the Gulf War, the Lorillard Tobacco Company in the United States added yellow ribbons, the traditional "welcome back" symbol for service personnel, to their Kent cigarette advertisements. This blatant attempt to link patriotism with smoking was reminiscent of the advertising themes in the First and Second World Wars. According to a Lorillard official, he "didn't know whether sales went up as a result" (*The CBC Journal*; 1 April 1991).
3. This is especially true for English language readers and less true for French language readers. Four of the top ten circulating magazines that anglophone Canadian women read originate in the United States and therefore are not subject to the Canadian tobacco advertising ban.
4. Another powerful script decision appeared in the children's movie *Jurassic Park* in 1993. The only smoker in the movie is also the only Black person in the script (a male computer programer). He smokes heavily throughout the movie and embodies the marketing thrust directed at the non-White American markets.

CHAPTER TWO

VALUES
THE MEANINGS OF SMOKING TO WOMEN

> What does smoking mean? How does smoking contribute to identity creation, image and emotional management? How does smoking reflect or direct experiences?

B obbie Jacobson's books on women and smoking (*The Ladykillers* and *Beating the Ladykillers*), published in the 1980s, gave some prominence to the voices of women smokers. Since then, several other feminist authors have focused on women's voices, suggesting that doing so will give meaning to the discussion about women and tobacco. Even so, women smokers are rarely, if ever, asked for guidance or input in understanding women's smoking, in setting policy or in developing programs.

This chapter documents some of these voices. Some of the women quoted here are women with whom I have spoken over the past eight years in both Canada and Australia, either in formal interview sessions, in focus groups or individually. Other quotes from women are derived from publications on related aspects of women and smoking.[1]

As a major part of my ongoing inquiry into women's smoking, I conducted in-depth, mostly one-to-one interviews with thirty-five women in Canada and Australia. I interviewed about one half of the women while they were residents of shelters for abused women. The other half were self-identified feminists active in a variety of fields. I recruited these women through networks of women's centres and women's shelters and through feminist groups. This strategy allowed me to focus part of my inquiry on how responses to questions about the meaning of smoking might be affected by being a survivor of woman abuse and/or by being a feminist (Greaves 1993).

A focus group was also conducted by me with First Nations women in Canada's North. These women were mainly smokers, with one ex-smoker participating, and were recruited through networks of community and health organizations. The members of this group, in addition to discussing their own smoking, delved into some issues regarding the general question of Aboriginal status and its possible relationship to smoking.

The women quoted in the following pages also come from many parts of the world. Their voices are recorded in the Herstories Project, which was carried out in 1993 and 1994 by the International Network of Women Against Tobacco (INWAT). An edited version of this material was published in 1994 by the American Cancer Society as Volume 19 of its journal, *World Smoking and Health*. Women in ten countries were interviewed by INWAT members,[2] using the same set of questions to guide the interviews. INWAT, formed in 1990, is dedicated to reducing and preventing smoking among girls and women around the globe. It is an organization made up of several hundred members with an elected executive. INWAT has little funding, other than support from various organizations.

The conclusions from these inquiries are only a beginning. Ongoing investigations must be undertaken with particular groups of smokers, especially those targeted by the industry such as young women, gays, lesbians and specific ethnic and racial groups. After having established some general themes of meaning through investigations to date, such ongoing studies will help to distinguish more finely the issues and meanings of smoking for particular groups.

I did not know what meanings women derived from smoking when I began this work nine years ago. However, I assumed that these meanings would be, in part, a reflection of women's life circumstances. I also thought that a central question regarding women's responses to patriarchal pressures could be applied to smoking. Are women smokers passively reacting to social and cultural pressures, actively resisting patriarchial inequality or a combination of both, at times? In other words, are women being passive or active as smokers?

The women interviewed for this investigation are not representative of all women. It is necessary to continue to extend such research into specific racial groups across various countries and cultures. In particular, it will be important to establish the impact of racism on not just smoking patterns and behaviour, but on the mechanisms of the global marketing of tobacco. It is also necessary to extend investigations to discover the particular impacts of, for example, sexual orientation, class, age, physical ability and ethnicity, as well as certain life circumstances or experiences such as abuse or imprisonment on the meaning derived from smoking.

While I attempt to develop theory in this book, it is not meant to explain the situation of *all* women smokers nor attribute meaning to women's smoking in groups and countries not yet examined. Rather, these inquiries offer us, as Marilyn Frye terms it, "clues" to "reading the landscape" (1983, xii). As she points out, the process of developing theory can be usefully informed in a variety of ways: "a single detail of an anecdote from one woman's experience may be exactly as fertile a clue as a carefully gotten and fully documented statistical result of a study of a thousand women... (ibid.)."

In charting the landscape, it is assumed that not every woman will be affected in the same way and that not all explanations offered or "clues" examined will apply to all women similarly or at all times. However, developing theory to explain behaviours or experiences rests on the assumption that it is possible to describe the forces that affect women, even differentially:

> ... if it is true that women constitute something like a caste that cuts across divisions such as race and economic class, then although the forces which subordinate women would be modified, deflected and camouflaged in various ways by the other factors at play ... we still ought to be able to describe those forces in ways which help make sense of the experiences of women who live in all sorts of different situations. (Frye 1983, xiii)

Notwithstanding assumptions such as these, "caste" status may often be determined by race where the powerful have an impact on the powerless in ways that cross gender lines. bell hooks makes this point in asserting that women (and men) share different experiences of "victim" status, and that the divisions of victim and oppressor are not neatly contained by gender but are largely affected by racism and class exploitation (1989, 20–21).

In this study, the women's interpretations of smoking are regarded as the essential starting point for developing theories of women's and girls' smoking. In this in-depth study of feminists and shelter residents, I wondered if these groups of women would describe smoking differently. Would the feminists see their smoking as arming them in their relationship to the world, and would the shelter residents see their smoking in relation to their victimization? Like any constructed categories, these two are artificial. Not unexpectedly, given the rates of violence against women, some of the feminists interviewed are also survivors of violence. Further, although not many of the shelter residents describe themselves as feminists, they sometimes express feminist views. The point in interviewing two identifiable groups was not to highlight their differences but to explore their commonalities.

Similarly, interviewing First Nations women smokers was an attempt to establish what overlap, if any, there is between their interpretations of their smoking and the two other groups' interpretations of their own experience. While women have different experiences and different locations in the world, exploring these differences probes the breadth of women's identities and feelings of agency specific to their circumstances. Because of the nature of the sampling techniques, the groups of women are not representative of their respective populations. For example, most, but not all, of the women in the Canada–Australia study are White. Most, but not all, speak English as a first language. Canada and Australia are very similar countries culturally and economically, with smoking regulations, laws and norms developing along similar patterns at similar rates.

The lengthy, detailed, semi-structured interviews were based on a set of ten questions[3] and record how women smokers make sense of their smoking. The shelter residents were specifically asked to consider if their abuse had any impact on their smoking and the feminists were encouraged to apply their tools of feminist analysis to their smoking histories and behaviour. In the focus group, the First Nations women were specifically asked to discuss if issues connected to Aboriginal status had an effect on their smoking. All of the women were encouraged to reflect on several identity issues related to their smoking. Any initial defensiveness and self-consciousness was usually based on preconceived ideas about the prevailing attitudes toward smoking and quitting.

Most women reported enjoying the discussions and interview sessions. The feeling was often voiced that being asked to think about smoking was also an opportunity to think about themselves. In addition, while quitting smoking sometimes became a topic of discussion, this was not a focus of the interviews.

Recording women's voices not only gives us otherwise unknown information about smoking, it also gives women smokers rare opportunities to talk about how this fundamental activity fits into their lives. The women smokers I met with were generally enthusiastic and appreciative of such an opportunity. Many women are occupied with thinking about others first and the value of their own lives, health and words often goes unacknowledged.

All the women interviewed in my in-depth study reported that no one had ever asked them to consider their own smoking behaviour in any meaningful way, and they themselves had not often considered their smoking behaviour in terms of its meaning or place in their lives. The failure to seek women's views on their experience is troubling. In the industrial countries, much is said and written and much policy and programing developed to deal with the issue of smoking, but asking women smokers for their thoughts is not common.

Five major themes emerge from the in-depth interviews in Canada and Australia. These are:

> **Organizing social relationships.** Women report using smoking to equalize, bond, distance, defuse or end relationships with others including partners, children and workmates.
> **Creating an image.** Women report using smoking to feel independent, different, stylish, accepted and, in a few cases, to stay thin.
> **Controlling emotions.** Women report using smoking to suppress or reduce negative emotions, anesthetize certain feelings or, less frequently, to allow positive emotions to emerge.
> **Dependency.** On this theme, women report using smoking as a source

of support, predictability or controllability.

Identity. The women interviewed see their smoking as grounds for guilt, tension, contradiction and a reason for self-castigation. As a result, the women reflect on their identity in light of their smoking.

All these themes were also mentioned by the First Nations women. Strong similarities exist between their interpretations of their smoking and those offered by the abused women and feminists. In addition, they felt that traditional usage of tobacco had little effect on their smoking decisions or behaviour, particularly for those who had lived all their lives in the North where no tobacco growing takes place. It is possible that the issues surrounding tobacco growing and symbolic and ritualistic uses of tobacco are more salient among First Nations people in more temperate zones. The First Nations women did, however, lace the issues of tobacco smoking into an analysis of the effects of alcohol and drugs on women and their children. Often, this led to the acknowledgement that alcohol was currently regarded as the more important problem for First Nations.

The issues raised by women, researchers and programers surrounding social relationships, image, emotion management and dependency have emerged in varying depths in other research. As a result, some of these concerns have already been incorporated into some progressive programs for women in countries such as Canada. In particular, the image-based reasons for smoking have received the most attention from tobacco policy advocates interested in affecting media and advertising messages, as well as those working with children and teens to ameliorate the effects of such messages. Dependency on smoking is often interpreted as a response to stress or as illustrating that women cope with daily life through smoking. The identity issues associated with smoking are only recently gaining more theoretical attention from researchers. Interestingly, in this study the identity issues garner the most attention from all groups when the women analyze the meaning of smoking in their lives.

While this study is composed of interviews with several groups of women, the substance of the women's remarks is remarkably consistent across the groups. In the Canada–Australia study, the abused women were more likely than the feminists to report that smoking offered them a site of dependence and control. However, the crisis-oriented nature of the abused women's situation may account for this. With this exception, the other themes emerge equally strongly in both groups of women. The differences lie in the sub-themes reflecting the varying ways in which smoking is usually used or interpreted by the women. Overall, though, the "search for differences," so often applied in research to distinguish abused women from others, proves fruitless in this inquiry. As expected, there is also little difference between women in Australia and Canada in the interview results.

However, more investigations with different groups of First Nations women, Inuit, Dene, Metis and Aboriginal women in other countries are required to further refine the analysis of differences and similarities.

The rest of this chapter deals with these five main themes, incorporating voices from the several sources mentioned above. In addition, various sub-themes uncovered in the in-depth interviews with women in Australia and Canada and the focus group with First Nations women are described, contributing to a deeper understanding of how these women smokers understand their smoking.

1. ORGANIZING SOCIAL RELATIONSHIPS

Smoking cigarettes is often a key element in social life. Smoking acts to equalize power relations between people, as a bonding agent between people or as a way to put distance between people. In some cases, women use smoking to actively defuse difficult moments in relationships by neutralizing tension or conflict.

Many people in industrial countries are keenly aware of the growing social disapproval and regulation of smoking. Women feel the impact of these trends on the development and organization of their social relationships in several ways. Because women are overrepresented as home-based workers and in caring roles around children, many spend much time alone in the domestic sphere. For women in these situations there is little distinction between work and leisure and they often use smoking to demarcate between these activities. In these cases, the regulation of public space may have less effect on women smokers. However, social disapproval of smoking is still absorbed by women, particularly when smoking impacts on women's reproductive labour such as during pregnancy. Social attitudes and patterns influence personal smoking behaviour, as illustrated by one woman's description of the sorts of situations in which she smokes:

> socially, if there's a group of friends, but if there's a group of friends with a predominantly smoking population then I smoke a lot but if I'm around friends that don't smoke a lot, then not a lot at all. [I'm] controlled, I guess, by other smokers around me. (Melba, an Australian feminist)

Smoking can be used to organize or even control social relationships. This functional aspect of smoking ought not to be overlooked or minimized as it provides a way for women to acquire or increase their power, or to neutralize power differences between themselves and others. Using smoking in this way can be a route to maintaining personal space and integrity in relationships. Both Graham (1993, 32–37) and Jacobson (1986, 94–95) describe women burdened by child care seeking temporary freedom through smoking by instructing children not to come near them for a few minutes while they smoke.

i) The Equalizer

Smoking sometimes serves as an equalizer between people when barriers need eliminating to allow for more meaningful interaction. Sharing the experience of smoking, particularly in an anti-smoking environment, can solidify, mend, build or even create social relationships. In workplaces where smoking controls are enforced, individuals often group together by smoking status during work breaks or dining. Social groups form that may previously have had no raison d'être and members experience a camaraderie based on sharing the smoking habit.

In describing the effects of smoking controls in her workplace, one woman states:

> the advantage to this is that people are out there [outside] from all different departments, people that I've never met before, or had conversations with before, and there is a whole new kind of social and intellectual business going on that people are in much closer contact than they ever were and actually decisions get made out there. . . . The poor nonsmokers are inside working their buns off and don't know what's going on. There's a certain amount of resentment among them about that. (Saskia, a Canadian feminist)

Smoking to equalize relations is also reported between women who have to relate to other women as clientele in various circumstances. A nurse working with drug addicted women believes that the fact that she smokes makes a difference to her relations with the women she deals with:

> it's saying "I'm on your level, you can trust me, I can relate to what you're talking about here," and so there's something that we have in common. They don't trust me. They see me as an authority figure and it's a really long process to win that over, win that trust over, and I think the fact that I smoke, I believe whether it's true or not, it gives me a feeling of helping the process. (Darla, an Australian feminist)

Sharing a cigarette break, a light or even social exclusion contributes to easing communication between people thrust together because of their roles. As staff, in particular, women see the sharing of the smoking habit as a key reducer of social distance. It increases ease and openness in communication and creates a way for other women to identify with them more completely. A worker in a battered women's shelter describes smoking with the women that she assists in the home:

> ... *you smoke if someone else is smoking, if you're talking to her and she lights up. [When] they have a situation like this [being in a shelter], they sort of make a connection with that.* (Win, an Australian feminist)

Some of the abused women use smoking as an equalizer with their husbands or partners. For some, sharing a smoking habit provides an opportunity to exert some power. Deborah, whose husband controlled the money and the purchase of cigarettes, has this to say:

> *if I didn't have any cigarettes, he didn't buy any for me so I didn't smoke. But I also wouldn't cook anything for him or do anything for him either. I would blackmail him until he bought me cigarettes, so he made sure I had cigarettes every day.* (Deborah, living in a Canadian shelter)

Barb, a woman whose abusive husband needed to quit smoking for serious health reasons, and offered her forty dollars to do likewise, refused to cooperate. She recalls:

> *I refused and thought "hope he dies," and [I] smoked more and he bought more and smoked more, [in order] to kill him.* (Barb, living in an Australian shelter)

ii) The Bond

Smoking can also build a sense of solidarity between people. Descriptions of warm moments sharing cigarettes with mothers, fathers, sisters and brothers are cited by many women from pro-smoking families. For some, family parties are sites of smoking freedom where their smoking habit is accepted and supported. According to Alice:

> *with my family, we buy cartons, we have smoke-a-thons.* (Alice, an Australian feminist)

Others smoke, and bond, outside of their families. For Alexia, who spent much of her truant adolescence at her friend's home instead of at school, smoking is an activity associated with acceptance and stimulation.

> *so all of us young women used to go around there and smoke our heads off during the day and talk and it was good and it was stimulating talk and I think that was the kind of home in terms of*

identifying with a group of very interesting people who also smoked.
(Alexia, an Australian feminist)

Adolescents often use smoking for bonding across divides. Gaining a sense of belonging is made easier and some barriers and stereotypes can be broken down. Helen describes her approach to integrating herself with some girls who were "less intelligent":

> *I think it was an attempt to prove to contemporaries lower down the "intelligence ranks" at school that the snobs (such as myself) could smoke just as well as everyone else. Meeting in the school lavatories for a surreptitious smoke helped to break down the unpleasant intellectual barriers between us at the time.* (Helen, quoted in Jacobson 1981, 30)

Many of the women smokers interviewed insist there are differences between smokers and non-smokers. Carla reports having consistently observed this and acted upon it as well:

> *smokers were always more interesting people . . . and all the partners I had were smokers as well.* (Carla, an Australian feminist)

She describes how her group of friends once contemplated quitting together and they asked:

> *well who do we know who's interesting who doesn't smoke? We were hard pressed to come up with anyone. It was a bit of a group thing, you know, let's just stay smoking and stay interesting!* (Carla, an Australian feminist)

The lingering historical perceptions of non-smokers as "good girls" and smokers as "bad girls" is often reflected. Alice recalls having lived with two non-smoking women for a while:

> *I couldn't handle that I wasn't allowed to smoke in the house with these two women. I couldn't connect with these women, they were alien beings, New Agers, extremely middle-class.* (Alice, an Australian feminist)

Some abused women recall rare moments of support or camaraderie with a partner when they shared a smoking habit. This constructed the set for co-operation or rare instances of mutual caring. Amanda describes instances of her partner rolling cigarettes at her request or sharing his lit cigarette with her.

> *[Once] I was almost sleeping, and I woke up because I was hot, and he was rolling a smoke so I said, 'Roll me one,' and he did.* (Amanda, living in a Canadian shelter)

Women often describe the simple pleasures of sharing something in common with their friends or partners. But bonding is possible only while both are still smoking. On considering quitting, Alberta worries that it might make her partner feel badly about herself for not also being able to quit, and worries that this might affect their relationship.

> *I know what it's like to feel like an outsider by having to [go outside for a cigarette]. [I wonder] what that means about my trying to protect the relationship by not wanting her feeling badly about herself.* (Alberta, a Canadian feminist)

> In my culture, smoking is not acceptable. For this reason, women have become closet smokers. I am a closet smoker who chooses where I smoke very carefully. I have a very special smoking realtionship with others like me—it's like building a partnership of loyalists who sometimes talk about giving up. (New Zealand woman interviewed by Sarah Thomson for "The Herstories Project" 1994)

In workplace or social situations, where smokers are now often cast out and thrown together in restricted smoking zones, there are powerful bonding opportunities. These opportunities create strong links between people who may not normally interact or converse. In fact, if a smoker becomes a non-smoker, this group identity is lost.

The solidarity of smokers can require conscious maintenance. Leora describes accepting a cigarette from a smoking acquaintance even when she did not really want one:

> *sometimes I'll have one with her when I wouldn't necessarily have one, to join her because I don't want her to think that I'm quitting or something . . . . [I do this to] support [the acquaintance] and one more isn't going to make a difference to whether I die or not.* (Leora, a Canadian feminist)

Smoking can facilitate more casual connections as well. Smoking in public is *"a great way to meet people."* Asking *"does anybody have a smoke?"* in a bar is a *"great conversation piece"* (Judith, living in a

Canadian shelter). But just as easily, Judith can end a conversation that she doesn't want to continue by leaving to go and get a cigarette. For Judith, negotiating a social situation such as a night out at a bar requires cigarettes.

> *I be-bop all over the place, having a great time, and I sit there and have a cigarette.* (Judith, living in a Canadian shelter)

This is just as true, if not more so, for teenagers. Some girls borrow cigarettes "to meet people and to break the ice" (McCracken 1992, 25). Jacobson (1981, 30) points out that, for heterosexual girls, "it is a way of saying, Hello, I like you, especially to boys."

iii) The Distancer

> *It's like it's my time . . . I was raised that that was relaxation. Mom was always allowed to take time to sit down and have her cigarette . . . it signalled, "Give Mom a break."* (Meg, a First Nations woman)

Women have often described how smoking can distance them from others in their lives, such as children, family members, partners or co-workers. Sometimes this distance is imposed by smoking policies or other pressures, sometimes it is deliberately established. The majority of the women interviewed use smoking to create distance in social situations. They report segregating themselves through smoking, often to get breaks from undesirable situations.

Women who are not members of pro-smoking families often clearly acknowledge the distancing function of their smoking with respect to family relations.

> *I don't have to sit inside with the family watching the television, talking rubbish. Quite often, I will go out to sit in the back garden and have a cigarette and somebody else will come out and there'll be a one-to-one interaction with that person. It's like holding court. It's like a little salon. People will come and talk to me . . . rather than being in the dynamic in the lounge room, with the telly blasting.* (Adelaide, an Australian feminist)

Adelaide welcomes this opportunity for distance and has long used her smoking to absent herself periodically from her family. For Alexia, the lines between smokers and non-smokers are very clear, and she acknowledges making social decisions based on this status in order to avoid internal conflicts about her own smoking:

> *I find myself not associating with friends and acquaintances that I*

ordinarily would, because they're non-smokers . . . I get tired of going to dinner parties at their place and going through the whole thing about should I step outside and have a cigarette? I haven't for a long time felt comfortable about smoking in a non-smoking household. . . . But I think basically it's guilt on my part. It's lack of self respect over the fact that I have this dependency. (Alexia, an Australian feminist)

[When] you're out with your friends or you're out for a good time . . . I started hanging out with non-smokers, so you felt like a real jerk smoking around them because they'd be . . . they never said anything of course but you knew it bothered them. (Louise, First Nations woman)

Sometimes smoking is used not so much to get away from something but to find something else. This is characterized as an emotional retreat:

often if I'm troubled about something, smoking can be a time for me to really think. It's something really comforting about making space and where I can quietly think through a problem that I have. (Alberta, a Canadian feminist)

I can remember when the children were very young, I learned that if ever I sat down, they immediately came and crawled all over me. So to try and have some peace, I used to prop my library book on top of the black fireplace, and have my cup of tea and cigarette standing up. That was the only time I felt I'd got some space on my own—doing my thing. . . That was the real highlight of the day. (Viv, quoted in Jacobson 1986, 93)

Judith uses smoking to cocoon herself:

I'm not going to look at you, I'm just going to sit and smoke my cigarette and I'm going to just keep on smoking and try and ignore you. (Judith, living in a Canadian shelter)

Smoking is sometimes a source of conflict or a mechanism of control for the abusive men referred to by the women interviewed. Actions of abusers, smokers or not, often reflect a need for control over women. Sometimes this is focused on the cost of smoking, other times on the woman's need for cigarettes. This can also be understood as a form of economic abuse as it involves the exertion of control over a person through deliberately and manipulatively limiting her money supply or access to resources. Activities such as these led Amanda to hide cigarettes to keep them in reserve.

> *He tries [to control my smoking], but it doesn't work because when I get some money I go out and buy a couple of packs and I hide one so if he just rolled a certain amount, I still have that too.* (Amanda, living in a Canadian shelter)

For Judith, another abused woman, the purchase of cigarettes was a bone of contention with her (smoking) male partner. Her partner earned and controlled their money and, through that, controlled her access to cigarettes. Even though he smoked more than she did, he would say she was smoking too much and should cut down.

> *I could never get money from him. Instead of buying two packs to last two days, he'd buy one pack.* (Judith)

Andrea had long noticed that her partner never allowed her to smoke more cigarettes than he did. He eventually controlled her intake completely:

> *if he felt like I should have a packet, I had a packet, if he didn't feel like I should, I didn't.*

She recalled how she sometimes

> *got to the stage where I collected the cigarette butts and emptied the tobacco out and rolled them.* (Andrea, living in an Australian shelter)

For Effie, a Greek immigrant who had been married twice to smokers, the control was even more overt. Although she had smoked for five years, she never smoked at home during either of her marriages because both men forbade her to:

> *the first one, I only lived with him for two months and no smoke. After I left him the first time, I went to my cousin's place and I smoked and I go back to my husband and stop smoking.* (Effie, living in an Australian shelter)

Annie describes the ultimate result of the exertion of control through access to cigarettes:

> *he never tried to take [them] away because he was a heavy smoker*

*too. I think it was the only thing we had in common. I can laugh
about it now ... we smoked the same brand. They were just there,
but God forbid if I ever smoked the last one ... I'd get it for sure.*
(Annie, living in a Canadian shelter)

Distancing between workmates, when desired, is also facilitated by
smoking. Some distance between smokers and non-smokers is often welcomed
by members of both groups. One woman, a medical worker, prefers being
with the smokers at her workplace because the companions she found there
are more to her liking. She is "at war" with her role as a medical person, as
she disagrees with the medical model and the values of her profession. As
a woman who knows the medical arguments against smoking, she expresses
her anti-establishment attitude by hanging out with the smokers. She secures
and maintains her political and social identity through smoking.

*[Smoking] isolated me from at least these jerks that I really felt I
had nothing in common with, except for a few of us and all of us were
smokers.* (Dayle, an Australian feminist)

The distancing function is reduced in situations where workplace[4]
smoking restrictions are already in force but, in worksites where the
smoking norms are still fluid, smokers can separate themselves from the
non-smokers either directly or indirectly. An indirect, conscious use of the
distancing function of smoking is evident in this nurse's description of a
staff meeting with male doctors.

*We may get into a discussion and I'll get up and smoke outside the
door and still participate. On one hand, that could be moving away
from the conflict, but it's not, it's really a power thing. I'll move
out here, but you have to sit there and listen to me. It's changing
the dynamic. The one who changes it gets the power. The one who
is changing gets watched. The time I would do it is when I want them
to listen to me, to see it my way ... and so I might move, so they
have to listen. I feel in a position of more control, it's useful, it's
manipulative, is what it is.* (Adelaide, an Australian feminist)

Direct distancing sometimes uses the danger of the ash, fire, matches
or smoke to deflect or repel various forms of social interaction. This is an
approach that mothers of young children often use. The smoke, the burning
tip, the matches or lighter, and the ash residue are all considered dangerous
for children, and reasons for leaving the smoker alone. This not only gains
the smoker distance, but smoking also becomes a relaxation technique and
a way to establish personal space.

> *I tend to say to the kids, "Just let Mommy have this smoke in peace"
> . . . it's something like it's my time that I've put down to thinking
> about what I want to do.* (Michelle, living in an Australian shelter)

Typical of many mothers of young children, Alexia reflects on her (adult)
children's earlier years:

> *I've felt very much at war with that role [mothering] since day one.
> [I was] using cigarettes to create a sense of space around myself
> to mark time for myself, to mark time out for myself, to mark a sign
> to be isolated.* (Alexia, an Australian feminist)

As Graham (1993) points out, such deliberate isolation can even prevent
physical abuse. A majority of the mothers surveyed suggested that smoking
prevented them from lashing out at their children."Sometimes I put him
outside the room, shut the door, and put the radio on full blast and I've sat
down and had a cigarette, calmed down and fetched him in again" (Mother
with pre-school child, quoted in Graham 1993, 35)

iv) The Defuser
Sometimes smoking can be artfully and deliberately used to defuse situations
or interactions. The interruptive and perceived protective aspects of smoking
are used to dilute conflict with partners, to decompress violent moments, to
buy time in conversation and even as a shield from potential abuse or danger.
Melba describes how she used the act of lighting two cigarettes when she
is feeling confused or is "losing ground" in a discussion with her partner.

> *I guess it's that I feel like I'm losing control of the issue, control
> of what I was saying and as if I'm being manipulated . . . usually
> in that situation I'll light two cigarettes and hand one to him which
> puts him in a position of having to stop what he's saying and to turn
> around and say "thank you," which gives me that little bit of power
> I guess.* (Melba, an Australian feminist)

She also feels that it gives her time to think as she goes through the
process of

> *finding them in your bag and finding the lighter and getting one out,
> fiddling around with the procedure of it all."* (Melba)

Judith describes several methods of defusing violent moments with her
abusive partner, including having a friend call regularly on the telephone,
going to the bathroom and lighting a cigarette. However, the cigarettes had

to be nearby for this strategy to work. On one occasion where she wanted to leave the room to get her cigarettes in the middle of a confrontation:

> *he grabbed me and said, "You ain't going nowhere, we're not done talking." That just really upset him that I wanted to leave and get my cigarettes. "You're not paying attention to me," and he ended up slapping me around. It was really upsetting to him. Whereas the other times where I had the cigarettes right there and [could light up and] break his concentration without him knowing it. I'm saying, "Yes, yes, I'm listening," then I light one up. I'm looking at him, listening to him, and yet he get's sidetracked by it. He doesn't know what's happening.* (Judith, living in a Canadian shelter)

Judith is convinced that lighting a cigarette in many situations has saved her from abuse:

> *I figured it worked a couple of times, if I have a cigarette in my hand or stuck in my mouth, then he's not going to hit me at least until I put that cigarette down.* (Judith)

In essence, Judith says smoking diverts attention:

> *if you're not smoking and you're trying to talk to somebody, they are looking right at you, you as a whole person.* (Judith)

Barb recalls that as a teenager, she used cigarettes for other protective purposes:

> *I always carried a . . . lit cigarette for protection . . . you can use it as a weapon . . . you stick that in someone's eye.* (Barb, living in an Australian shelter)

The defusing of violence is a key use of smoking for abused women in the inquiry. Not only does smoking deter, deflect and distract, but the smoke is a screen around the self. For Victoria, a feminist recounting an earlier abusive relationship, the decision to interrupt a fight with her former husband by having a smoke preserved her dignity:

> *I could hide, by looking down, or behind the smoke . . . I could hide my fear of him.* (Victoria, an Australian feminist)

48

2. CREATING AN IMAGE

Image creation through smoking is central to the promotion and marketing of cigarettes. For some teenagers it is assumed that being "cool" and grown-up are key image gains achieved by smoking. But how may women see smoking contributing to their image? By the time smoking is an established habit, image may be understood in a fuller way. Many women smokers incorporate an image of themselves into their subjective interpretation of the meaning of smoking.

This image is affected by both external and internal pressures.

> In public ... I'll whip through [a cigarette] and put all evidence out of sight as quickly as possible ... we are portraying something we shouldn't .... In private, there is no 'image' being portrayed. In private, it is a time to reflect over a nice cigarette. (New Zealand woman, "The Herstories Project," interviewed by Sarah Thomson 1994)

There are several aspects of the images supported by smoking: independence, difference, symbolism and ritualism, conformity and, occasionally, aiding weight control. As a social statement or a fashion prop, a psychological statement or a message, smoking is clearly loaded with meaning. Cigarettes can help to project images and reflect values.

i) Independence

Many women report that as young women they perceived smoking as an adult, risky, autonomous, powerful behaviour. Regina, who had experienced smoking Camel cigarettes with her stepfather from age ten, describes how she introduced other girls to smoking:

> *I was really cool because I was the initiator. I had a lot of power and that was my reason for being included in the world* (Regina, a Canadian feminist).

She recalled the wonderful stories about "worldly girls showing other girls cigarettes" (Regina).

Judith derives a lot of courage from smoking cigarettes:

> *I don't think I could be as brave if I don't smoke. I'm pretty brave when I have a cigarette in my mouth. I light up a cigarette and get all the courage in the world.* (Judith, living in a Canadian shelter)

Several women describe smoking, particularly in front of their parents,

49

as a turning point or declaration of independence.

> *I guess I would've been eighteen before I was allowed [to smoke in front of them] . . . when I was sixteen, my father was sitting at the kitchen table just kind of blowing smoke in my face and laughing . . . 'cause he knew I smoked, but I wasn't allowed to smoke around him.* (Donna, a First Nations woman)

According to some smokers, smoking is at times their sole identifiable independent behaviour. After describing her complete inability to make decisions about her personal appearance or anything else in her life, Marina says:

> *. . . my smoking was basically about it [the only decision I made] as far as personal appearance goes.* (Marina, living in a Canadian shelter)

ii) Difference

Many women reflect that when they first began to smoke in earnest, usually during their teens, smoking made them feel "cool," "tough," "adventurous," "rebellious" or "interesting." Cigarettes were a significant prop in achieving these attitudes or postures.

> *I just wanted to be cool, being cool was always important to me in the rebel part of me. It was also wrong, so I did it.* (Alberta, a Canadian feminist)

As an adult, Alberta says:

> *[if] I want to be unapproachable or cool or whatever . . . it's hard to do that if you don't have a cigarette in your hand.* (Alberta)

> *We were big wheels when we had cigarettes in our hands, we felt great. We thought we were pretty cool, that was the big highlight of the day, going to have a smoke.* (Annie, living in a Canadian shelter)

Saskia recalls her smoking initiation as an adventure, allowing her to mix in environments "different" from her familiar ones. After continuing to smoke off and on during her early teens, she went away to university and in

> *first year I learned all the dangerous vices and it was wonderful.*

*I learned to drink, I learned to smoke, I learned to screw, I didn't
have to play with dolls. I learned everything I had to do in my mind
as being free and grown up.* (Saskia, a Canadian feminist)

Asked what she liked about smoking as a young teenager, Ivana
says:

My mother didn't like it so I liked it. (Ivana, living in an Australian
shelter)

Judith smoked as a teen because it was "cool," but as an adult she links
smoking to being "interesting." She describes going to a bar with a non-
smoking friend:

*she just sat there all night, just drinking her drink and did nothing
with her hands. [She] just looked like a bump on a log. And she
didn't talk to anybody, she never did get to know anybody.* (Judith)

Judith concluded that someone like her non-smoking friend, looks boring.

*I don't want to be like that. I want to be me. It's [smoking] just
become so much a part of me and my personality.* (Judith)

*The image that comes to mind is "good" people . . . you know
[something like] good people don't have fun. But I don't feel that
a smoker has a hard nature, or a really bad attitude.* (Claire, living
in a Canadian shelter)

For women on the margins of a society such as Dari, a Black woman who
is an Angolan refugee to Australia and living in a shelter, the interesting
aspect of smoking is intrinsic to the behaviour:

*smoking is exciting, this is an interesting new country, many people
smoke wherever you go.* (Dari)

As adult women, the independence theme shifts to emphasize more
"autonomy" and "risk-taking." For those women who feel marginalized by
anti–smoking norms, this independence can transform into feelings of
defiance and difference. This leads to important identity considerations
when one is contemplating quitting, as Alberta reveals:

*we are the outcasts and we have our own bonding because of that
and I would miss that.* (Alberta, a Canadian feminist)

iii) Symbol and Ritual

The rituals and symbols connected to cigarettes and smoking are an important part of the smoking image. Much of this can be attributed to the values deliberately transmitted through woman-specific tobacco marketing and advertising. But much smoking ritual is developed as a cultural practice and, for girls and women, the ritual is definitely a gendered activity. For Amanda, smoking style is important. She is careful not to smoke while trying to do other tasks.

> *I'm not the type that I can stand seeing anybody with a cigarette hanging out of their mouth.* (Amanda, living in Canadian shelter)

> *... [O]ne of the reasons why I don't smoke on the street [is] because my mother was a lady and she smoked but she never did in public.* (Claire, living in a Canadian shelter)

For Judith, the worst cigarette is a hand-rolled one. In discussing the expense of smoking, she rejects the idea of ever rolling her own

> *because they're disgusting. It doesn't look good, for one thing. Those things are really horrible.* (Judith, living in a Canadian shelter)

The initiation ritual can be very memorable. Most smokers have vivid memories of their first cigarette.

> *I can remember it as if it were yesterday. It was neat. She was teaching me how to smoke and you go "Like this" when you are smoking, and "Like this," and it didn't take me long to get used to inhaling. . . . It was relaxing and being relaxed was such a great feeling. It made me feel good and as I got older and the more I smoked, then I could handle the inhaling part a lot better and it was a breeze.* (Roberta, living in a Canadian shelter)

Adelaide recalls her high-school smoking experiences as a "ritual."

> *There were other kids that I would meet, ten minutes before school. . . it was a specific crowd who would meet and come into the toilets and smoke and it would be one before school, one at recess, two at lunch time, one as soon as lunch came out and then you'd go to eat your lunch and then go back and have another one. One at recess, and then sometimes you'd go down the lane for one on the way home.* (Adelaide, an Australian feminist)

A much more brutal ritual is recalled by Regina, who was introduced to smoking by her incestuous step-father.

Once he had achieved orgasm . . . he would sort of create me as an adult . . . and he would give me a cup of tea, or later on . . . a drink and then for the first few years of my smoking he would give me a cigarette.

Regina interprets her smoking as

taking back some power which doesn't feel so alien from the experiences of many school girls getting together with cigarettes . . . and wanting to feel more powerful, more independent, more old and more in control of their lives. (Regina, a Canadian feminist)

The ritual of smoking cigarettes usually involves a smoking style. Particular styles of smoking are identified by some of the women interviewed. Such activities as "drawing," inhaling, blowing smoke and holding cigarettes in certain ways all add to the images being projected. The consciousness of these activities varies but, when acknowledged, are described in positive ways.

Michelle explains:

I liked [smoking] . . . just enjoyed it. I liked the feel of smoke going down, I liked breathing it and I used to love watching it flow in. . . . It just fascinated me to think what you could do with it and it just kept fascinating me and I used to blow smoke rings. I don't like lighting up a smoke and putting it down and leaving it in the ashtray. I like to smoke it. (Michelle, living in an Australian shelter)

Melba recalls:

a nice lighter. I had one, I lost it . . . it was quite attractive. It was a gold one. That was the good part of lighting a cigarette, using that . . . the sophistication, the gold, classy, elegance. Just possessing something like that made it look good. Also the action of smoking, I really like the exhaling, blowing out the smoke . . . the drawback[5] is like taking in these feelings and having them continue. (Melba, an Australian feminist)

Another woman, a Chilean immigrant to Australia, in reflecting on cigarette advertisements, observes:

> *They have good-looking people, beautiful, white and sexy.* (Mercedes, living in an Australian shelter)

Unlike Mercedes, few of the women express any conscious recognition of being influenced by cigarette advertising. However, many are aware of the "lightness" and length of various brands and sometimes manipulate their brand choice around a cigarette they perceive to be "healthier." Win's recollection of brands from age fourteen is precise.

> *Cameos when I was fourteen. Then after that, Rothmans, du Maurier, Vantage, Players, Players Light, and just recently, I went down to Matinee Extra Mild to try to be able to quit. I guess I'm conning myself when I say, "If I get onto a lighter cigarette, it's not as bad."* (Win, a Canadian feminist)

> *Well I'm really glad I don't smoke Players or Export-A because they have the tackiest packages there are. I'm not kidding. I think du Maurier has nice packages.* (Catharine, a Canadian feminist)

Barb remembers choosing brands based on others' choices:

> *the lady across the road had the soft pack. I used to look at what other people were smoking more, and get that. Everybody had Marlboro and Alpine. In hospital, it was Drum [loose tobacco] . . . but I tried to put tips in the Drum. Peter Stuyvesant soft pack was my favourite, it was very attractive.* (Barb, living in an Australian shelter)

As for memorable rituals, when rolling her own cigarettes as a child, Barb

> *would spike cigarettes with cinnamon and [have] hallucinations.* (Barb, living in an Australian shelter)

No matter how benign, the idea of giving up some of the rituals associated with smoking is virtually impossible for Meg:

> *I've tried that [visualizing myself a non-smoker]. I've seen myself going out for coffee with a friend and sitting there with nothing in my hands . . . just going and talking . . . I'm so used to putting the cigarettes out on the table, "Oh, have one if you want. Here, want*

a smoke?" Smoking, it just seems like talking . . . I've tried to picture myself just saying, "Oh no, thanks, I don't smoke" . . . and I just can't see it. (Meg, First Nations woman)

iv) Fitting In

. . . [B]efore it was cool to smoke, and now when I'm older, it's cool when you quit. (Louise, a First Nations woman)

It is often presumed that peer pressure has a significant effect on the initiation of smoking by children and young people. The women in this study reveal many examples of acquiring and maintaining social acceptance by friends, family and co-workers through smoking, in some cases long past adolescence. They describe using smoking to achieve conformity and approval.

Some describe buying friends by offering cigarettes or having impressed their peers with their smoking freedom at home or with their families. As adults, several women who are outsiders or marginalized for some reason smoke as a route to acceptance or solidarity. Roberta, a woman who had been excluded from groups at school, shared cigarettes with a new girl and gained some social acceptance:

one day if I didn't have the smokes, she got the cigarettes, and if she didn't have them, I always did. Because when I was out, she always had some, and when she was out, I always had some . . . she was a girlfriend of mine, when she was new I got to her before any of the other students could, because I wanted her to get to know the real me instead of having other people tell her stories about me. (Roberta, living in a Canadian shelter)

[Smoking is] . . . sociable and friendly with my friends in the refuge. I buy cigarettes sometimes in the blue box, because I am embarrassed to ask my friends for them. (Dari, living in an Australian shelter)

Mercedes, whose smoking increased after arriving at the shelter, feels:

people smoke to be sociable, in control. Maybe I'm just a copycat. But you go anywhere people are smoking . . . so what's the point in quitting if you are sociable? (Mercedes)

Almost every woman I played sports with were lesbians and we all smoked and nobody was worried about whether they were going to be slim. Obviously, it had nothing to do with physical activity because we were active. We all smoked. I can't think of anybody that didn't. (Leora, a Canadian feminist)

v) Weight Control

A final aspect of image creation through smoking is weight control. Much advertising directed at women dwells on this theme and encourages the linkage of slimness with smoking. Indeed, nicotine intake can control weight, primarily through speeding up the metabolic process. In this study, however, a minority of women mention this use of smoking and none of the feminists raise this theme.

For three of the women, though, smoking cigarettes is seen as a deliberate appetite control mechanism. Amanda consciously smokes instead of eating.

> *I don't usually eat breakfast. First thing in the morning, I roll out of bed and I light a smoke. I'll end up having a sandwich for supper or lunch and a lot of times at supper I'll end up smoking instead of eating because I want to lose weight. I figure if I smoke I won't eat as much.* (Amanda, living in a Canadian shelter)

Vera has a long history of obsessively controlling her food intake and weight. She eats no breakfast, a liquid food supplement for lunch and a light supper. When asked if she could visualize herself as a non-smoker, she says "No." Her main concern is avoiding weight gain. Maree, who formerly was morbidly obese and had a surgical stomach stapling, states:

> *if I get nervous, I'll have a cigarette instead of going to the cupboard to get food, I'll do that. It's like a drug addict. I'm a drug addict if I have cigarettes and there's people that are food addicts and they eat food, food, food. When they get nervous they go the cupboard and they eat.* (Maree, living in an Australian shelter)

3. CONTROLLING EMOTIONS

Suppressing negative emotions through smoking has been reported by some women for several years (see Jacobson 1981). Diverting anger and frustration with children is only part of this pattern. Cigarette smoking is also useful for controlling emotions such as fear, sadness, rage and confusion in a variety of situations. According to Mrs. S., "Getting angry hurts others. When I smoke, I feel a release in my whole body from anger and tension. The cigarette won't hurt anybody but me" (quoted in Jacobson 1981, 34).

> *I found the more confused my life became, the more I smoked. It was the older I got, the more confused I got.* (Marina, living in a Canadian shelter)

Related to this is the generalized control of worry, tension, boredom and other "upset" feelings. Part of the pattern includes anesthetizing feelings, using cigarettes to limit, delay, temper or de-intensify them.

> *My cigarettes were a barometer of how I felt. If I was tense, I smoked more cigarettes. . . . There was a predictable consistency in my self–destructive behaviour. If I was feeling relaxed and good in relation to myself, I would probably cut down on the number of cigarettes I smoked. It all seemed to hinge on how I viewed myself.* (Claudia, quoted in Jacobson 1986, 87)

In general, the abused women often report using smoking as an antidote to acute stress. Smoking can also be associated with creating positive emotional outcomes by allowing a feeling of creativity or providing pleasure and relaxation.

Women smokers may manage emotions with cigarettes when social expectations preclude more externalized displays of feeling. Aggression, directness and assertiveness are not generally part of female socialization. In addition, the emotional management of others' feelings, particularly family members, is often assigned to women.

i) Squashing Negative Feelings

Suppressing emotions by smoking can be conscious and deliberate. Sometimes, though, it is only upon reflection that a woman realizes that this is a major use of smoking in her life. Either way, many women bluntly state that they would rather smoke than express certain emotions, and that this is a necessary choice. If she weren't smoking, Marina said, she would

> *probably be chewing everybody's heads off.* (Marina, living in a Canadian shelter)

There are several other aspects of containing emotion:

> *I don't want to be miserable, I don't want to bark at people. Because I like to be nice.* (Vera, living in a Canadian shelter)

> *If I didn't smoke I would be angry and irritable. I don't want to be like that . . . I don't want to be growling at everybody . . . at my family . . . if I didn't smoke I'd be lashing out at people . . . there's so many other things that you have to control.* (Victoria, an Australian feminist)

> *[Smoking] helps me control my emotion, helps me not cry if I don't*

want to, not yelling when I want to explode, like with my child, I know I should not take my aggression out on her. It's kept me safe when I've been upset . . . (Darla, an Australian feminist)

I know when I've been angry I've reached for a cigarette when I haven't been able to deal with it at the time . . . like the person isn't there, or it's at a time I can't do anything about it . . . I know I've reached for a cigarette. (Donna, a First Nations woman)

Not surprisingly, the abused women interviewed report slightly higher rates of using smoking for supressing emotions. For Judith, her level of consumption of tobacco is related to the escalation of abuse in her relationship.

I was almost up to two packs a day. It definitely increased. Before this started [the latest escalation of abuse], I only smoked half a pack a day. (Judith, living in a Canadian shelter)

Some of the incidents described by the abused women illustrate this suppression of emotion very well. Judith could clearly recall often reaching for a cigarette instead of talking back when in a violent confrontation with her abusive partner.

When you're scared, I want to say "Leave me alone," but so many times I just sat there and he could really be yelling at me. My mind is saying, "I want to reach up and punch you right in the mouth," but I'm too scared. Now if I didn't have a cigarette to break that, I don't know how I would handle that other than really getting brave and hoping that I have a good shot, and reaching for the ashtray and decking him with it. (Judith, living in a Canadian shelter)

This strategy is not unique. After describing how she started smoking during an argument with an abusive (ex)husband, Pauline surmises that:

It worked. Whatever it was that it was supposed to do, it worked. It calmed me down [and stopped me] from throwing an ashtray at him. (Pauline, a First Nations woman)

Many of the women in this study say that smoking allows them to avoid risking the effects of releasing negative emotions or even having to discuss such feelings. Anticipating more arguments, abuse, unpleasantness, damage or just a generalized guilt for causing discomfort, they smoke instead. Conscious or not, this reflects both the limited options they have and the relative powerlessness women often feel in interpersonal relations.

ii) Dispelling Tension

Many smokers connect "being upset" and smoking. As the abused women were more recently dislocated by the events in their lives, more of them report either using cigarettes to assuage their emotions or even relapsing in reaction to emotional upheaval. However, about one half of the self-described feminists and the First Nations women also discuss using smoking in this way.

> *Usually it's just feeling a lot more pressure around work or personal issues, just when I start to feel pretty gruesome, I'll start to smoke more.* (Alberta, a Canadian feminist)

> *Often [smoking] is a release of tension, a release of letting it all out, getting rid of it all.* (Melba, an Australian feminist)

> *If I'm distressed or upset I smoke more. If I'm worried or any of those sorts of things, I smoke more.* (Victoria, an Australian feminist)

> *[If I'm] fighting with somebody, if I'm really worried about someone I'll start smoking a lot. You know, on better days sometimes I'll just forget about it . . . .* [Lana, a First Nations woman)

Smoking helps to control stress responses such as tension and worry. Marina likens the feeling to eating when hungry:

> *I feel my body starting to tighten up and as soon as I light it my body just starts to relax. It's basically the same as food. My body feels uncomfortable until I eat and then when I eat I feel better.* (Marina, living in a Canadian shelter)

Roberta, who lived in a constant state of fear of abuse and walked on eggshells much of the time, says:

> *I was so nervous and scared and I smoked constantly. Smoking calms me down, it kind of eases me . . . my hands start shaking, and the first thing I do is grab a cigarette, and it goes away when I take a puff. So the more I smoke the more I calm down and get more relaxed . . . same when I'm nervous, I don't feel as nervous.* (Roberta, living in a Canadian shelter)

> *Stress, depression, everything. If I'm upset I smoke more. If I'm worried, I smoke more.* (Judith, living in a Canadian shelter)

Some abused women relate their smoking to distinct events. Michelle describes her response when her estranged husband called and tried to reclaim the children:

> *that was it then, I just smoked and smoked and smoked heaps.* (Michelle, living in an Australian shelter)

> *[Smoking] is a way to relax, I guess. I get so mad and so upset and I get off the phone here after my husband is already screaming his head off and I go right to the dining room table and I smoke cigarettes.* (Vera, living in a Canadian shelter)

Jessie describes her relapse which occurred the night she left her abusive husband:

> *I could have done without it [smoking]. . . . It was probably something to take my mind off it or just because I was very anxious. It was sort of the first thing I thought of.* (Jessie, living in an Australian shelter)

Links between smoking and emotional state are often abundantly clear:

> *When we [my husband and I] were happy I didn't smoke much but when things went bad I smoked twice as much.* (Ivana, living in an Australian shelter)

> *. . . [A] lot of it [my smoking] is boredom and a lot of it's if there's a tense situation, then I know I need a smoke.* (Claire, living in an Canadian shelter)

> *It's pretty boring around here, there's nothing to do so I smoke.* (Jessie, living in an Australian shelter)

In a similar vein, Regina, a worker at a shelter for women, states that for both workers and residents:

> *smoking is really a behaviour connected with the crisis shelter.* (Regina, a Canadian feminist)

Trish and Lana also reported that smoking was a behaviour connected with their workplaces:

> *you feel good when you get up, and then when the day's going*

downhill, you start smoking (Trish, a First Nations woman)

If I'm having a good day at work, then I won't smoke that much, but if everything seems to be going downhill for a while, then I'll smoke at work. (Lana, a First Nations woman)

iii) An Anesthetic

Less often, smoking is used by women to delay an emotional response or to limit feelings about a person or situation. In this sense, cigarettes are medication.

I think the other thing it does for me which I don't know if it's good or bad, it tempers my feelings . . . [I'm] a little bit frightened about the intensity of my emotions if I don't smoke. [Smoking] de-intensifies my emotion at the beginning so that I can decide how I want to express it. (Alberta, a Canadian feminist)

For Claire, these functions of smoking were illustrated whenever she had tried to quit. Only then had her abusive husband commented on her smoking:

Quite often he would just walk into the house with a pack of cigarettes and throw them on the table because he knew it was going to be a tough situation. Because he didn't like the way things were, the anger. If one thing was bad, that [smoking] was the anesthetic, because I was more verbal when I wasn't smoking. It was a good excuse to open up the gates and let all the disgust and hate, all the emotions, surface. (Claire, living in a Canadian shelter)

[Smoking] . . . helped to soften the blow, helped me cope with him and his bashings. (Barb, living in an Australian shelter)

Sometimes that was through simply delaying her own response:

I had to have a cigarette so I could do what I had to do, so I could think, before I [did] anything. (Barb)

Ivana's understanding of the tempering effect of her smoking on her emotional response to her husband is considerably more clear:

[Smoking] made me not so tense so I felt like killing him. [Smoking] prevented me from cutting his throat. (Ivana, living in an Australian shelter)

iv) Enhancing Feeling

On occasion, some women report that positive feelings are enhanced by smoking. Creativity, clarity and productivity are connected with smoking:

> *I use smoking in two ways. One is for the hype, particularly in the mornings or when I'm at work. I use it as a stimulant so that my brain goes; plus, I use it to reward myself . . . so you find yourself, I've got to think, gotta think, gotta have a cigarette.* (Sidney, an Australian feminist)

Similarly, Jessie describes:

> *the first puff of the cigarette would sort of wake you up and you know you were alive, physical[ly] and mental[ly]. You can sort of feel it in your lungs. Just sort of makes you feel good. . . .* (Jessie, living in an Australian shelter)

Saskia and Michelle both notice improvement in their concentration:

> *so it's like a thinking tool, or has been, and I'm finding now we're in a smoke-free environment at work that I don't think as well. It takes me much longer to do things. Sometimes I go outside to have a cigarette just so I can think. . . .* (Saskia, a Canadian feminist)

> *[I]t gets me in a different frame of mind because I'm thinking and I'm thinking and I'm thinking harder about what I want to think about rather than having a hundred thoughts rushing through me here . . . I can concentrate on one.* (Michelle, living in an Australian shelter)

For Darla, positive emotions are enhanced through smoking:

> *After the birth [of my child], I was so full of achievement, I really wanted a cigarette . . . a reward, making space for me, after all that had happened to me. [I also smoke in] emotional times, when I feel really good . . . after I've made love, to finish off something lovely.* (Darla, an Australian feminist)

4. DEPENDENCY

Apart from the compelling addiction to nicotine, some women also describe an emotional dependence on smoking. When asked if they could visualize themselves as non-smokers, the extent and power of this dependency often emerges. As Graham has noted, smoking is a particularly important resource in times of crisis (1994, 120). This is especially true for those with little money or opportunity. For women enduring unemployment, poverty and other disadvantages, smoking is both a refuge and a resource for coping. In essence, those with other options for seeking social or emotional support may be more able to visualize themselves as non-smokers.

Not surprisingly, then, when dreams are dashed and options close down, smoking offers a critical support to smokers: "I smoke because everything I have wanted has been ruined. I haven't got anything left now" (Pregnant lone mother of a two year old, living in a British refuge; quoted in Oakley 1989, 321)

When dependency issues are raised, considerable feeling is evoked in smokers. Smoking is seen by some smokers as a support, as comfort or a source of companionship. It is also a source of predictability in the lives of some women, giving dependability, security and anchorage. And last, the malleability of smoking is valuable to some of the women interviewed. Smoking is controllable, available and ultimately an intimate act. On all of these themes, the abused women in this study are more likely to attach importance to smoking. While dependency is, overall, the least often explicitly mentioned theme, its naming affords the most salient and powerful testimony. For in this realm, the intensity of women's links to smoking is revealed.

i) Support

Smoking is perceived as an important source of comfort and companionship and, in some cases, the line of protection between life and death. Smoking can offer protection emotionally as well as physically. Smoking soothes and comforts in many and varied situations. For example, when fear, harassment or tension can be escaped or reduced through smoking, then it becomes an important link between the reality and psychosocial peace. Cigarettes become companions, offering comfort and friendship.

> *My cigarettes have been more consistent than any people in my life.* (Carla, an Australian feminist)

> *. . . unless I run out, I've always got my smokes with me.* (Amanda, living in a Canadian shelter)

Judith describes her feelings toward cigarettes, particularly in moments of violence against her:

> *we were arguing and as soon as he started raising his voice . . . I got a cigarette . . . I needed something . . . I got something so that I'm not alone. I can't turn to anything else here, so I have to have*

a cigarette. (Judith, living in a Canadian shelter)

I think smoking has been a comfort and it still is. (Win, a Canadian feminist, reflecting on twenty-five years of smoking)

Such sentiments directly affect the possibility of becoming a non-smoker. Amanda answers "No" when asked if she could imagine not smoking. After some effort, she adds:

I'd probably be on Valium. I was talking about quitting smoking and he [a doctor she had visited] said, "Don't, she'll be on Valium all the time." I said, "Forget it, I'll just smoke." (Amanda, living in a Canadian shelter)

If she could not smoke, she says: *"I'd probably end up dying."* Asked what would make her quit, if anything, Amanda says: *"When I die."* The only exception she can make, after some thought, is if she had a child who needed food and she didn't have enough money for cigarettes. (This occurred once before in her life, and for two weeks she had gone without cigarettes in order to buy food for her baby.)

Win, who had once tried to quit, describes smoking as her comfort:

it still is, because whenever I think about quitting, I think, "Oh, my God, I can't." I only tried it once and I didn't smoke for one day and I was almost a basket case. (Win, a Canadian feminist)

I don't think I'd ever be able to do it [quit smoking], unless I was dying and I couldn't lift my hand to pick up a cigarette, then I'd probably give it up. (Ivana, living in an Australian shelter)

When I gave up I had to stay busy. But at the end of being busy, what do you do then? . . . Sometimes I [would] just cry for hours . . . just this gap in your life. Grief. (Carla, Australian feminist, reflecting on a former attempt at quitting)

For a few women, depending on cigarettes is freeing; it is an exercise in "letting go" and allowing themselves to be supported, comforted and held together. Barb, who has difficulty sleeping due to memories of night-time sexual abuse, describes her smoking habit: *"[at night] smoking was a comfort."* (Barb, living in an Australian shelter).

ii) Anchorage

Cigarettes are also described as a source of predictability. Some women emphasize the permanent availability of their cigarettes and the dependability they represent, often in marked contrast to other parts of their lives. The reliability and consistency of cigarettes is the key to security for many women and a real deterrent to quitting smoking.

Graham (1993) points out that this is enhanced for mothers living in disadvantaged circumstances where time, money and leisure opportunities are scarce.

> *I just gotta have cigarettes by my side 'cause they're the only stable thing in my life . . . Just not having them is the hardest thing. I won't smoke them, but I've gotta have them 'cause they're my best friend"* (Young pregnant mother, quoted in Graham 1993, 36).

> *. . . [C]igarettes have been with me for most of my life. It's been something that's been really consistent and something that I can rely on.* (Alberta, a Canadian feminist)

Sometimes, facing the strength of this dependency is startling. Barb, whose life had been full of violence since her childhood and who began to smoke at thirteen, states:

> *they're [cigarettes] like a partner. They're the most dependable partner I've had. Cigarettes are my best friend . . . they're the most dependable thing, it's frightening to think of it.*

Tightly hugging her packet of cigarettes to her chest, she continues:

> *looking back over my life, cigarettes have helped me, they're there whenever I was scared, they were with me if I was nervous.* (Barb, living in an Australian shelter)

Several of the women note that cigarettes have been a companion for a large part, if not most, of their lives. Cigarettes are often described as more worthy than other people, especially by abused women.

> *As far as I can see you can't count on a guy because they are not always there, kids aren't always there. . . . I'd say it's [smoking] my security. Because they [cigarettes] are always there.* (Amanda, living in a Canadian shelter)

> *I can't rely on somebody to make me feel secure like I do with a*

cigarette. I can't rely on people. The only person I can rely on is myself . . . and a cigarette. (Judith, living in a Canadian shelter)

For some women whose lives may have been devoid of predictability and security, the passivity of the cigarette and the constancy and security of smoking is very important. Visualizing life without smoking is extremely difficult for many of the women interviewed, particularly some of the abused women. For a few of the women, imagining this was simply impossible.

> *I would have had a total nervous breakdown by now if I hadn't had something to live on, like something when you've got nowhere else to turn. . . . I need something or I'm going to crack and that cigarette's there. If I hadn't had that, if I hadn't smoked I don't know what I would have done. I just can't imagine.* (Judith, living in a Canadian shelter)

When women do confront this intensity of feeling, the issues of dependency have to be examined. Women are then invariably forced to deal with some central questions of their own identity.

> *It frightens me, it actually frightens me, to think of not smoking. I'm not sure why. . . .* (Victoria, an Australian feminist)

(iii) Control

Cigarettes are concrete, consumable and controllable. Because of ongoing inequalities, many women in general are powerless relative to men. Even more powerless are women who are poor or marginalized for some other reason. Women describe valuing smoking because of their ability to completely control the cigarette. While insignificant to some, this capacity is important when women are deprived of tangible control over other aspects of their environment.

For women in crisis situations or experiencing material disadvantage, the value derived from controlling cigarettes may be even more important. Some women describe how the cigarette is always available and could be smoked whenever they desired. They often feel in control of this decision. Women can direct the entire activity of smoking with a passive, comforting and dependable partner, the cigarette.

> *I guess it's something orderly. There's a routine to it . . . it's something to stick to. It's something I'm familiar with. It's something I know how to do very well because I've done it so many times before. I guess also the fact that I've made a decision by myself that*

I'm going to have a cigarette now and I'll go through a process of doing it and I don't need to rely on anybody else, unless you run out of cigarettes, of course. When you've got your own, you don't need to rely on anybody else to implement the decision that you've made . . . you can carry that through. (Melba, an Australian feminist)

For a teen mother interviewed by Hilary Graham, smoking is "the only thing I do for myself, isn't it? I have to do things for the baby and my husband, but smoking is about the only thing I can do for myself" (Young mother, quoted in Graham 1993, 36).

. . . (smoking) is something I'm doing just for me, and nobody can take it away. (Deborah, living in a Canadian shelter)

Part of it I think is something that is destructive and a lot of it is something that just I feel like I can have control of. It's my choice. My husband could tell me to quit smoking every day if he wanted to and it didn't do him any good. Like I say, basically, it's just something I could decide on. (Marina, living in a Canadian shelter)

Annie defines her smoking as the only legacy of her relationship:

you know, I didn't have a whole lot else except my cigarettes, that was it. What have you got with a house full of kids, and a maniac for a husband . . . it was just something I had that he couldn't take away from me . . . that was the only thing that was left out of the marriage. (Annie, living in a Canadian shelter)

Graham's study of disadvantaged smokers illustrates that seeking control through smoking is not limited to adult women but may develop early as a response to uncertainty and deprivation.

I live from day to day not knowing if the lights would be turned off, 'phone disconnected or we'd have food to eat. I know it just wastes money when I buy cigarettes, but I don't drink or use drugs. Smoking is the only thing I do for myself. I don't have money to go to the movies or skating rinks like other kids. (Young female smoker, quoted in Graham 1993, 20)

5. Identity

I'm me when I smoke . . . I need to smoke in front of people. The cigarette forms a part of me and my personality. . . . It accompanies me everywhere, in good moments and bad. (E.B., a Spanish journalist who smokes forty cigarettes per day, interviewed for "the Herstories Project" by Dolors Marin Tuya 1994)

Issues of identity and smoking are gaining more attention. There is considerable pressure to refine tobacco programs and policies (in industrial countries) to better address women who are still beginning or continuing to smoke in the face of increased knowledge and anti-smoking pressures. This interest in identity issues is overdue. Most women smokers, when interviewed at any length, eventually focus on identity issues. These issues comprise the richest source for understanding how women feel about smoking and how society contributes to its perpetuation.

Practically all the women with whom I have ever discussed smoking consider their smoking, to some degree, problematic. Some of this understanding is due to the pressures of anti-smoking norms and legislation, which increasingly marginalize smoking and smokers. Many adults began smoking in a more pro-smoking era and are betrayed by their addiction when asked to quit. Most smokers (according to research and survey data) want to quit, but attempts at cessation prove extremely difficult.

More striking than the difficulty faced in dealing with external pressures or physiological constraints, however, is the considerable tension experienced over maintaining their smoking in face of their *own* feelings and attitudes about smoking (and about themselves). While some women may see that smoking helps them cope with a variety of oppressions or intrusions in their bodies or lives, this does not prevent them from frequently defending or explaining their smoking as if it were a failure and weakness *in them*.

Identity issues are the most frequent theme discussed by all categories of women interviewed in the Australia–Canada study. The First Nations women also stressed this aspect of smoking, although not in ways specific to the Aboriginal identity. Overall, several aspects of identity were identified. Some women feel guilty about expense, health risks (to self and others), environmental effects and (sometimes) about contributing to the tobacco industry.

There is also tension regarding the meaning of smoking and female identity; does it indicate being in control or being controlled, addiction or rebellion, traditional female role behaviour or breaking free? These pivotal questions gnaw at women smokers. Linked to this tension is much contradiction. Could one feel both autonomous and dependent? Are women smokers actually disempowered by the industry or by the addiction? Could a former smoker cope with the power and perfection implied if one quit? The final theme raised is self-castigation, reflecting a perceived inability to quit which feeds a feeling of weakness and self-destructiveness.

i) Guilt

Guilt about smoking often centres on the effects of smoking on others: children, partners or others in the environment of the smoker.

> *Guilt is one of my prime motivators [explaining her wavering smoking habit] . . . recognition of the truths about health risks [played a part] but I had never quite internalized the risk to myself . . . [it's] easier to apply those risks and warning as the risk I bring to others [by smoking around them].* (Catharine, a Canadian feminist)

In different ways, the women measure the quality of their love for others by their smoking behaviour.

> *What will make me undertake that pain is if I care enough about this other human being.* (Catharine, a Canadian feminist)

> *I know for sure that if I was to quit smoking right now it would have to do more with my feelings about other people than it would about my appreciation for how this would benefit my life.* (Regina, a Canadian feminist)

This can also work against quitting. Alberta implies that she would feel guilty even if she quit, as it would mean leaving her smoking partner behind:

> *since I'm so good at taking care of other people in relationships, I think it's partly what I've been doing here.* (Alberta, Canadian feminist)

Children, babies or pregnancies and breast-feeding feature prominently in guilt feelings for many women:

> *I tried to quit when my son was nine months old. He had had his first asthma attack when he was three months old, and I desperately wanted to quit for his sake. I went [without smoking] for one day and almost died.* (Win, a Canadian feminist)

> *I can remember breast-feeding and smoking even though I thought, "this is wrong."* (Sidney, an Australian feminist)

> *I think once the pregnancy starts advancing I might give it up . . . I'll probably end up starting again once the baby's born but I don't know.* (Alexia, a pregnant woman living in an Australian shelter)

[Quitting]. . . . It's something I've given serious considerations to . . . I really started seriously thinking about quitting smoking. I have two asthmatic children. (Marina, living in a Canadian shelter)

This concern extends to others' children as well:

My roomate is pregnant so, . . . as soon as that baby's there, I'll probably start smoking outside . . . . (Lana, a First Nations woman)

For some women, expense contributes to guilt about smoking, particularly when money is short.

It's too expensive to smoke anymore. That's strongly influencing me to quit. It's $150 per month. (Marina, living in a Canadian shelter)

Most of the women consider smoking unhealthy and self-destructive, but a few of the feminists also consider the purchase of cigarettes a contribution to the multinational conglomerate "enemy."

I am psyching myself up to become a non-smoker, not because of the horrifying information I have read on health hazards, but because I object violently to helping finance the tobacco industry. It's another corporate exploitation of women, and as a feminist that really offends me that I'm not smart enough to say, "Fuck you, I know what you're doing, and you're not going to fuck me around" . . . but the motive [for possibly quitting] at the moment is the stupid tobacco companies and the money they take . . . it's actually more than just another drug problem, it's a conspiracy. (Darla, an Australian feminist)

. . . [O]ne of the corporate factors that has had an effect on me was finding out which companies were South African based so that I could boycott politically on that basis. (Saskia, a Canadian feminist, discussing a recent brand change)

ii) Tension: What Kind of Woman *Am* I?

Dependency, security, disgusting. (Alberta, a Canadian feminist, describing what smoking means to her).

The women express tensions which directly centre on their conception of the female (and their own) identity and which include several aspects. Are women who smoke "addicts," "rebels" or both? (Resolving this is not easy for women claiming either description. There are certain implications when (re)claiming the "rebel" identity and continuing to smoke under that banner, or claiming the "addict" label and continuing to smoke because self-control could be more legitimately given up to an addiction, especially one as profound as smoking tobacco.) Does smoking indicate passivity or pro-activity in creating identity? Is smoking feminine? Is it connected to traditional female behaviour? And last, does smoking control the woman or do women control their lives through smoking?

For a feminist, smoking often contradicts the politics of empowerment that circumscribes a feminist world view. When a feminist critique is applied to the tobacco industry and women's smoking, the result is a tense contradiction.

> *You do all the things as feminists. I feel like I've done everything from the feminist perspective, from a very early age, in order to not buy into a whole lot of things. Like twenty to thirty years later, you're spending a fortune and suffering socially and emotionally and it's real hard to feel good about yourself as a smoker. It's just impossible. It's crazy.* (Sidney, an Australian feminist)

> *I actually think I would be a lot healthier emotionally because I wouldn't be trying to manipulate my emotions. I'd be forced to deal with them more directly.* (Alberta, a Canadian feminist, discussing not smoking)

Other feminist interpretations of smoking focus on self-analysis and recognition of responses to pressure.

> *I'm saying I'm not perfect. I need something to help me too, I get stressed too. I need to cope too, and yet I'm still okay, in society . . . in line with the feminist ideals of showing your vulnerability. I could rationalize it like that, I don't think that's really true but I could rationalize it.* (Darla, an Australian feminist)

> *The smoking thing is tied very much to a . . . regaining of self that may never have been there in the first place that is about taking myself seriously and caring for myself as only I can ever know how to do that. I am not yet there . . . and no one else can do that for me. It's a resolution of a lot of stuff.* (Carla, an Australian feminist)

> *I think the thing about smoking is when people say "How can you smoke? You should know better (as a medical worker)." When*

people talk about quit programs, it makes me feel like lighting up a cigarette. (Dayle, an Australian feminist)

Some of the abused women reported feelings of wanting to resist:

I enjoy it and I'm stubborn. (Judith, living in a Canadian shelter)

. . . if somebody told me to quit, I probably wouldn't. I went out with one guy that didn't smoke and it only lasted a couple of weeks because he was right on my case all the time about smoking, and I just said, "Look, if you don't [smoke], that's fine, I do, too bad." (Amanda, living in a Canadian shelter, describing an incident thirteen years prior)

For some of the abused women, tension about smoking often reflects feeling like failures at the heterosexual marriage ideal. This raises questions about femininity. Crushed ideals become merged with their continuing to smoke. Some express bitterness and disappointment at the realization that following the rules and role of traditional femininity did not necessarily lead where they expected it would:

A Beaver Cleaver⁶ family, like you see on T.V. . . . a fairytale, like the Beaver Cleaver family. I'd have a little girl, and I'd be married, and he'd be working and I'd be working too, and I'd have a beautiful house . . . there'd be no problems . . . or if there were, we'd deal with them at a nonviolent level. We'd be a family the kind you see on T.V. shows, they work out their problems. (Roberta, living in a Canadian shelter, describing her ideal circumstances for being a non-smoker)

When we first started dating, I never smoked when I was with him unless we were out in public, but if we were alone somewhere together, I wouldn't smoke. He really didn't like it and quite often he would say kissing you is like licking a dirty ashtray. [I said] . . . don't kiss me then. He did not and he's always hounded me about my smoking. (Marina, living in a Canadian shelter)

The issue of being in control or being controlled through smoking is a critical one. While women may often start smoking in order to appear in control, the eventual irony is that smoking also controls them.

Cigarettes do control me, I guess, but I control them. (Barb, living in an Australian shelter)

Part of it [smoking] I think is something that is destructive and a lot of it is something that I feel I can have control of. But, I don't really control my smoking. (Marina, living in a Canadian shelter)

If you say you're giving up smoking then you have to control that, too. To me, that's all so hard. (Victoria, Australian feminist)

. . . [T]hey are controlling me and it is a sort of vicious circle situation and I guess I only look at the side of it that I want to. (Melba, an Australian feminist)

Darla's comment on the control issue reveals her awareness of her inabilities:

I feel like I'm controlling my existence [through smoking]. Academically, I know that I could have control without smoking, but I have to find a way of doing that. Losing it feels threatening. (Darla, an Australian feminist)

Carla reacts to anti-smoking sentiment and her sense of being controlled:

I'm actually hiding my smoking now like I did when I was a girl . . . I've gone full circle, or gone backwards. (Carla, an Australian feminist)

When faced with imagining how life would have to be for her to be a non-smoker, Amanda says:

no problems. No food. I'd have to be real skinny, well not real skinny, what I was like, I'd be happy. No mother around. No men.

To replace smoking, she would need:

somebody that's going to be there, not a guy that will say, "Oh, I'll be there no matter what," but they're not. Was that possible? No. Because they can be there sometimes but not all the time. They aren't always with you. (Amanda, living in a Canadian shelter)

Jessie also realizes it is unrealistic to attain a problem-free life which would set the stage for quitting. She perceives her crisis at the shelter as an opportunity.

[I] must [now] assume responsibility for my life and that includes

and implies quitting. (Jessie, living in an Australian shelter)

iii) Contradictions

> *I want to be free of everything. To me smoking is like a ball and chain.* (Marina, living in a Canadian shelter)

If women see smoking as undesirable, but make no move to stop, a contradiction is experienced. Sometimes smoking is disdained, but women are still drawn to cigarettes and this creates a split between their thoughts and behaviour.

A First Nations health worker, Lana, feels a conflict between her role and her smoking. Much of her work centres on providing better health care to First Nations women and men, and making sure opportunities to access health care are made available to her people.

> *People look at you like, "Hey, you're a health worker and a chain-smoker?" . . . and it's no good.* (Lana, a First Nations woman)

A number of the women interviewed view smoking as undesirable:

> *I sure hate smoking and I wish that it was just so easy to quit . . . [but] as soon as I start to think about it, my body just tightens up.* (Marina, living in a Canadian shelter)

> *I've read all the literature, I've seen movies, I've taken care of people. A nurse should know.* (Vera, a nurse who had looked after terminal cancer patients, living in a Canadian shelter)

> *I have one part of me sort of saying, you're crazy, this is ridiculous and on the other side, it's well, I'm under a lot of stress, I do this because I enjoy this, I'm an adult. I can make these rational decisions if I want to. It's a lot of game playing within yourself and defending it to yourself and to other people at times.* (Melba, a nurse who had looked after emphysema and lung cancer patients, an Australian feminist)

> *I hate it. I hate that it has affected my health very much, and I developed asthma two years ago, and I know that the smoking only complicates it. I hate the amount of money I spend. I hate that I'm addicted to it. I do feel controlled by it and when I try and quit I hate all the things I go through trying not to smoke. I hate the smell on clothes and stuff. I hate that. Most times I hate the taste and I don't*

even like how it feels. (Alberta, a Canadian feminist)

I just think that this is really a stupid hobby.... (Saskia, a Canadian feminist)

There is nothing worse than a woman with a cigarette hanging out of her mouth ... [Smoking is] dirty and cheap. It doesn't look nice. It makes you smell, it makes your clothes smell. I hate it. (Maree, living in an Australian shelter)

For many women the contradiction is acute when they smoke and don't enjoy it:

it's rare for me to enjoy a cigarette and that would have been true for my whole history of smoking and there are lots of times that they make me sick and I continue to smoke.... All cigarettes taste bad, some cigarettes taste worse than others. I make a [brand] choice based on what I know doesn't taste as bad as other things. (Catharine, a Canadian feminist)

Smoking is repugnant, because it does control and dominate some aspects of life ... I don't think I've enjoyed smoking a cigarette for fifteen years. I haven't enjoyed the feeling. [But] I can't imagine being a non-smoker. It wouldn't have fit in with a lot of other things I've done, or still am doing. (Carla, an Australian feminist)

It's a dirty, rotten, filthy habit. (Louise, a First Nations woman)

... sometimes it's really embarrassing and I really want a cigarette and finally I'll have one but I'll feel really embarrassed. I don't enjoy it anyway. (Melba, an Australian feminist, on smoking in an anti-smoking atmosphere)

Where am I going to be? I'll still be around, probably, hopefully. Where will I be, out in the back, out behind the shed like my Dad was when he was growing up? (Vera, living in a Canadian shelter, wondering about the coming of a smoke-free society)

The First Nations women interviewed have thoughts about alcohol use and smoking and the relationship between these problems. Meg, who ended her addiction to alcohol many years before, feels that while drinking caused her to express negative behaviour, smoking is a signal of her relaxation:

75

It's not illegal, and I'm not misbehaving . . . you see, I can rationalize so well . . . but I couldn't rationalize my way out of the alcohol any more. (Meg, a First Nations woman)

And she went on to say:

Well, it's better than Valium.

Collectively, the health issues surrounding Aboriginal women's alcohol use and fetal alcohol syndrome are seen as a priority in the North where the First Nations women live and work.

We're at the point where we're talking about fetal alcohol syndrome. People have to think about quitting drinking, never mind quitting smoking. Quitting smoking is the lesser of the two evils. (Pauline, a First Nations woman)

There are also some ambivalent feelings about becoming a successful quitter. The image of health summons up images of perfection and powerfulness for many of the women interviewed. Despite the apparent attraction of this, some women feel ambivalent about becoming a non-smoker. Some women worry about feeling too "good," too perfect or too powerful if they should succeed in quitting. These contradictions highlight questions about empowerment and disempowerment for women smokers.

I can say I've toyed with the idea if there was an easy way of doing it. I'm not overly impressed by that image . . . a healthier image. I do get bronchial problems in the winter. Most smokers always get that, it goes along with smoking. Everybody told me how everything tastes better, you appreciate air more, you don't smell like smoke and your clothes don't smell. That's nice, almost too good, maybe I'm not a good person. Maybe somewhere down the line I deserve to be a bad person. (Claire, living in a Canadian shelter)

. . . [E]motionally I would be healthier . . . I would have to deal with things differently, I wouldn't have smoke screens so I'd have to find other ways to do it. I think there's a part of me that is afraid of being too successful. I've been quite successful anyway in my life, and the more successful I am the more people expect of me . . . It scares me. (Alberta, Canadian feminist)

. . . [S]moking is my uncontrol, my proof that I'm not completely controlled and it's reassuring, that is. (Saskia, a Canadian feminist)

Alice describes a period of three years, when she was seventeen to twenty years old when she gave up smoking, adopted a pure, organic diet and discovered politics:

> *I was disgusting. I was hideous. I'd be preaching to my whole family and all my friends and I think I was just trying to find my identity anyway. I don't want to be a Puritan again. I couldn't stand it.* (Alice, an Australian feminist)

Now a resumed smoker, Alice speculates that, for White people like herself, the perfection surrounding quitting smoking is about superiority.

> *[I've been] taught I'm superior to other people. If I get together with a bunch of aboriginal people, I'll smoke up, I'll drink up, I'll talk . . . there's something that brings us all together with that smoking . . . with all not wanting to be absolutely perfect. I don't want to be that perfect.* (Alice, an Australian feminist)

iv) Self-Punishment

> *. . . I've used giving up smoking to say to myself, "This is how I am and I accept myself . . . I'm strong now!* (M.J., former smoker, Spain, interviewed by Dolors Marin Tuya for "The Herstories Project" 1994)

The women often castigate themselves for not being able to quit. What does this say about identity? Am I really weak and self-destructive?

> *I get very angry with myself at times because it makes me feel as if I don't have the strength that I want to decide today, that's it, no more smoking.* (Melba, an Australian feminist)

> *The thing is I'm too intelligent to smoke, it damages my health, my child, is physically unattractive and a stupid thing to do.* (Darla, an Australian feminist)

> *I feel really uncomfortable when I'm sitting on the sidewalk having a cigarette. I feel like people are looking at me.* (Lana, a First Nations woman)

The abused women also comment on how they feel smoking highlights their weaknesses:

The image that comes to mind is good people. (Claire, living in a Canadian shelter, describing her image of successful quitters)

When asked if she wanted to be good:

>*... No, I guess not. I don't know whether it goes back to the "I don't deserve to be good" or, you know, somewhere in there good people don't have fun.* (Claire,)

>*I feel stupid. I have to go [to the smoking room] to have a cigarette, everybody looks at me ... I don't care, I'm going anyway ... when you stop and think how ridiculous it is [my devotion to smoking], it amazes me how a grown-up person can be that ridiculous ... I know how stupid it is, but I still smoke.* (Annie, living in a Canadian shelter)

>*Sometimes I think, gee, you're disgusting. I really do. It's already half way through the day and now I've already smoked thirty smokes and I've got to say tomorrow, you're not going to smoke as much.* (Michelle, living in an Australian shelter, discussing the various health effects of smoking on her body)

>*I'm spineless. I don't really feel good about the fact that I'm still smoking. I go through a battle all the time between my [sports] training and my smoking.* (Alberta, Canadian feminist)

WHAT DOES SMOKING SAY?

Many adult women smokers end up not liking smoking because it highlights their weakness or lack of control. However, they welcome the physiological effects of smoking which feed the addiction to nicotine. As young women just starting to smoke, the opposite had often been true. The sensory impact was unpleasant but the psychosocial benefits were welcome. During those early years of smoking, women experienced pleasurable feelings even when their younger bodies struggled with the effects of nicotine.

The voices of women smokers in this chapter are drawn from several countries, sources and different groups of women. The in-depth interviews with abused women and feminists in Canada and Australia are described in some detail to probe the commonalites of thought and analysis applied to smoking by women in different circumstances. The abused women more often focus on the present in their descriptions and questions, while the self-described feminists reflect the ability to ponder their smoking in a larger framework. Even so, the themes described by the women are similar with only slight variations in emphasis.

Identity issues are dominant for all of the women smokers. They ask themselves, what does smoking say about me, especially in a world of constantly changing rules about smoking? Did I buy into a habit encouraged by the culture and now find myself too weak to resist? Or, am I a resister, and this form of expression is my rejection of being too good, too obedient and too oppressed? Am I controlled by smoking or am I controlling life by smoking? As we have seen in this chapter, these questions are as engaging to women smokers as they are to theoreticians.

NOTES

1. Some such publications include several articles and a book by Hilary Graham: *When Life's a Drag: Women, Smoking and Disadvantage* (1993); *Her Share of Misfortune: Women, Smoking and Low Income* (1993) by the ASH working group on women and smoking in the UK; and Bobbie Jacobson's books, *The Ladykillers* (1981) and *Beating the Ladykillers* (1986).

2. The interviewers were: Sarah Thomson, New Zealand; Nobuko Nakano, Japan; Vera Luiza da Costa e Silva, Brazil; Monika Salu, Estonia; Charlotte Chasteen, USA; Rosini Karsono, Indonesia; Grace Burnside, Northern Ireland; Mira Aghi, India; Dolores Marin Tuya, Spain; and Nancy Tesha, Tanzania.

    The questions, detailed below, were followed with numerous probes that focused on each woman's and each country's situation. In all cases, the questions were addressed at both micro and macro levels.

    1. How does tobacco affect your environment?
    2. How does tobacco play a part in your economy?
    3. How is tobacco represented to women in your culture?
    4. How does tobacco affect the health of women and children?
    5. How does tobacco affect your life?

3. The guiding questions were:

    1. Can you recall your first cigarette?
    2. What do you like about smoking?
    3. What do you dislike about smoking?
    4. When and where do you smoke?
    5. What changes in your smoking patterns have taken place over the years?
    6. Do you ever smoke in place of doing (or saying) something else?
    7. Have you ever thought of quitting?
    8. Have you ever quit? In what circumstances?
    9. How do you feel about smoking? What does it mean to you?
    10. Can you visualize yourself as a non-smoker? What would your life have to be like?

4. Even before workplace smoking controls became popular, smoking breaks ("smokos") were used in industrial countries to delineate the workday and get distance from work, machinery, customers or even the actual worksite itself. The "smoko" tradition was particularly important for the workers in situations where they had little control over their work, such as in factories. These workers grew to experience the smoking break as a welcome change in the workday and a key to the social interaction available at work.

5. The action of reinhaling the same smoke.
6. A famous American 1950s situation comedy, based on a patriarchal, domesticated-mother family structure.

CHAPTER THREE

COSTS
WOMEN'S EXPERIENCES WITH TOBACCO

> Women pay the costs of tobacco growing and smoking as, for
> example, consumers of tobacco and advertising, workers, caregivers
> and, of course, ill and dying smokers.

It is clear that smoking has value for some women but what are the costs?
It is difficult to unbraid all of the overlapping effects of tobacco. Apart
from becoming statistics, women who smoke are also caregivers and
workers. Similarly, women who do not smoke are also deeply affected by
the availability, production, promotion and use of cigarettes by others. This
chapter examines these threads separately in order to highlight the issues
while acknowledging the interrelatedness of the experiences.

WOMEN AS CONSUMERS
Women in various parts of the world have consumed tobacco for several
centuries but cigarettes have been popular among women in industrial
countries for only several decades (see Chapter One). In the Third World,
5 to 10 per cent of women currently smoke cigarettes. Although these rates
are rising, they are still far below the rates in industrial countries which
range from 20 to 45 per cent (Chollat-Traquet 1992, Chapter 1).

Traditional uses of tobacco are still prevalent in many Asian, African
and Middle Eastern areas. Where smoking is considered unacceptable for
women, tobacco chewing by women is often widespread. In India, for
example, women have long chewed pan which is a mixture of tobacco plus
several spices (Chollat-Traquet 1992, 6–7). Some Indian women have also
traditionally smoked cheroots, bidis and chutta. Recently, educated urban
women in India have been turning to cigarettes as a mark of sophistication.

In Southeast Asia and the Pacific Rim, similar increases in cigarette
consumption are only now occurring. Even in industrial Asian countries
such as Japan, the rate of women's smoking has remained low despite high
rates of smoking by men.

Although the acceptability of women's smoking was contested throughout

the industrial world during the late 1800s and the early decades of the 1900s, marketing tobacco to women had an early start in both North and South America. Evidence of "female brands" of cigars and pipe tobacco exists, and marketing to these women was commonplace during this period (Cook 1991, 9–10).

Marketing cigarettes to women occurred somewhat later. By the 1920s, the tobacco companies subtly began to shift their attention to the female market. In Britain, Craven A ads featured images of "flappers," denoting liberation in order to attract women smokers. Players ads were more direct, using the line, "Players Please—the Ladies too," to develop the female market (Jacobson 1986, 43). Australian cigarette ads were directed at women a little later, using more subtle images of women passively consuming the smoke from men's cigarettes (ibid.).

In North America, however, lasting and influential trends were set in woman-focused cigarette advertising by Lucky Strike's 1928 ad with the caption, "Reach for a Lucky Instead of a Sweet," establishing a durable link between smoking and slimness for women. Further testimonials on the effectiveness of smoking as a dieting technique from society women, athletes and actresses buttressed this campaign (Marchand 1985, 99).

At the time, candy manufacturers objected to this clearly competitive copy but succeeded only in moderating the language. The reworked advertising includes the following copy: "Pretty Curves Win! When tempted to over-indulge, Reach for a Lucky instead" (Marchand 1985, 101). Despite or even because of the wrath of the candy manufacturers, the Lucky campaign was very successful and stands as the original seed of the many contemporary weight control campaigns such as the 1990 Virginia Superslims ad with the caption "Fat Smoke is History" (Taxi 1990). While purporting to promote a new cigarette with 70 per cent less smoke than other 100 millimetre cigarettes, the copy includes: "It took Virginia Slims to create a great tasting ultra thin cigarette that gives you more than a sleek shape."

In the intervening decades, the tobacco industry has created many

woman-focused products and advertising campaigns across the industrial world. The increase in women's smoking over the decades suggests strongly that smoking rates are linked to the careful and attentive advertising and sponsorship strategies developed since the late 1920s.

Prior to 1920, many cigarette advertisers in North America and elsewhere had been careful not to target women directly in their material, due to remaining negative attitudes and the fear of a prohibitionist backlash (Ernster 1985, 336). But by the late 1920s the advertisers stressed the stylish and trendy aspects of smoking. At the same time, women were indirectly featured in tobacco advertising focused on men, such as the Chesterfield ad which says "Blow Some My Way" and pictures a woman looking longingly and sensuously at a man and his cigarette. This was not only a symbolization of female desire, but also a comment on the nascent passive smoking lobby. Some brands were promoted using the testimonial; Lucky Strike used supportive quotes from socialites and famous women such as Amelia Earheart to promote their product. Other testimonials included doctors, movie actresses, or radio personalities.

By the 1930s and 1940s, a more unisex approach to smoking was evident in the advertising, reflecting women's growing emancipation and changing roles in the industrial countries. Women's suffrage, women's participation in the war effort and women working in non-traditional occupations set the stage for the elaboration of the smoking equals freedom theme. Advertising in these decades continued to stress testimonials and to "personalize" the product. The Lucky Strike advertisement points out: "When all else fails I'm your best friend." It was a better friend than others, because "in personal tragedies, a Lucky stands you in good stead" (Marchand 1985, 358). Also, during the 1930s, Luckies were promoted as nerve-calming agents, and were marketed to both men and women as an aid in crisis situations (ibid., 99–100).

The most successful American advertising messages promoting cigarette use by women have expressed overtly feminist messages. The Virginia

You've come a long way, baby.

Short cigarettes are made for men.

FAT cigarettes are made for men.

Stubby cigarettes are made for men.

Virginia Slims is made long and slim just for you.

Slims series featuring modern women, with sepia photographs of their imagined female counterparts of years gone by, is a familiar example of this. Most of these ads utilize the slogan: "You've come a long way, baby." Virginia Slims created this campaign in 1970 with the second-wave of the modern Western feminist movement (White 1988, 127), thereby capitalizing on the mood of rebelliousness which was cresting among White middle-class feminists at the time. This approach is not confined to North America. In India, in 1989, a brand of cigarettes called "Ms." was launched to develop the Indian, urban, educated female market. The result is a simplistic but durable conceptualization of women's smoking as an act of liberation.

WHAT DO THE ADS MEAN?

The culture of advertising has moved through several stages in North America since the 1920s (Leiss, Kline and Jhally 1990). Between 1920 and 1950, products were often associated with values and taste; between 1950 and 1970, products were "personalized" and marketed to appeal to individual feelings. Since 1970, "lifestyles" have featured in the presentation of products with cigarettes being no exception. Sometimes threads of older approaches are also apparent in current advertising.

Since the 1920s, the attachment of symbolic meaning to cigarettes has been the preferred technique of marketers in several countries, permitting the sale of much more than the cigarette. The advertising industry's techniques in manufacturing demand have been widely discussed in the last three decades. Most important are those techniques which attach symbolic meaning to products.

By 1920, workers in North America were beginning to be seen by marketers as consumers as well as producers. Their industriousness was previously the prime interest of many capitalists.[1] Levine (1983) describes corporate support for the temperance movement. While opposition to smoking was less frequent, Henry Ford stood out in his preference for non-smokers as workers and in 1914 he published an anti-cigarette book, *The Case Against the Little White Slaver* (Troyer and Markle 1983, 37). Ford also employed sociologists in his company prior to 1920 to make his workers more industrious. Their advice included the proscription of tobacco use (Lasch, 1979). Marketers recognized that this newly identified group of consumers would need to be educated in the "culture of consumption." Such "education" was often presented as fashion and progress, replete with the illusion of freedom where women, in particular, could express their autonomy through the consumption of goods which advertising promoted.

As Lasch aptly points out, women may have been freed from one yoke of paternalism (patriarchal authority), only to have it replaced by the "new paternalism of the advertising industry, the industrial corporation and the state" (Lasch 1979, 140). The marketing of cigarettes to women illustrates this shift.

Simon Chapman, an Australian researcher, contends that tobacco advertisements "mediate" between the cultural contradictions surrounding smoking. Advertising counteracts the many negative concerns about smoking (disease, addiction, etc.) with images about the ideal: images of health and freedom and symbols of distinction and prestige (Chapman 1986). For example, ads that feature images of outdoor scenes, fresh country air, athleticism and successful heterosexual relations serve to counteract notions of odour, poor health and (hetero)sexual insecurity. This not only lessens the awareness of health risks but also supports consumers in starting or continuing to smoke by constantly reducing their ambivalence.

FINDING MORE CONSUMERS:
NEW PRODUCTS, CHILDREN, MINORITIES AND THE THIRD WORLD

By the 1970s, tobacco companies were facing a market crisis in the industrial world because of the declining male market. To secure a future market, they began actively targeted women and children, later progressing to specific ethnic and racial groups, and then to Third World countries. In the trade journal, the *Tobacco Reporter*, a 1982 article, "Targeting Women," was one of many clearly calling for a new and aggressive strategy aimed at the female market segment.

> Women are adopting more dominant roles in society; they have increased spending power, they live longer than men. All in all, that makes women a prime target as far as any alert [European] marketing man is concerned (Rogers 1982, 8).

85

Other points made in several of these trade journals remind marketers of women's increased job-related stress and women's apparent dedication to smoking once they take it up (Jacobson 1986).

While the advertisements[2] would come to reflect this strategy, product development also shifted to account for this new industry focus. Filter tips had been introduced to cigarettes in the 1950s as the industry's response to early health scares, but the product innovations specifically directed at women and children were low-tar, low-nicotine, "light" cigarettes. In addition, cigarettes took on slim shapes to reinforce the equation between smoking and slimness, and the 100 millimetre cigarette was introduced as a woman's cigarette. As Davis points out, advertisements for women's brands appear prominently in *Weight Watchers* magazine (1987, 729).

The development of these new products was primarily intended to overcome the physical and physiological barriers to smoking faced by women and girls : that of lower tolerance to the nicotine in tobacco and a resulting tendency to be unable to smoke (or learn to smoke) regular cigarettes. Silverstein and Kozlowski (1980) suggest that the availability of low nicotine cigarettes facilitates the initiation of smoking in teenage girls by reducing toxic reactions. Despite manufacturers' claims that they are not targeting the youth market, it is clear that attracting this market segment to the smoking habit is crucial to future sales.

Men are much more likely than women to use high-strength cigarettes (United States Public Health Service 1980) and women more likely to use low-strength cigarettes. However, low-tar cigarettes are perceived to be less of a health threat or "safer," and those smoking them may not be as highly motivated to attempt cessation (Stevens, Green and Primavera 1982). Miller (1985, 316) concludes that the "less hazardous" cigarette is a "deadly delusion" and a "hypothetical construct." Indeed, as Jacobson points out, while low-tar may reduce the cancer risks associated with smoking, it does not reduce the risks of cardiovascular diseases, the primary morbidity associated with smoking (1986, 61).

The introduction of low-tar and low-nicotine cigarettes may have had a dual impact: it may ease the initiation of the child or female smoker, and reduce the motivation to quit once addicted. Chapman contends that the tobacco industry has repositioned the consumer's choice from one of smoking or not smoking to one of low or high nicotine cigarettes (Chapman 1986, 130). This shift creates a profitable illusion as it leaves room for addicted smokers to make a proactive decision to reduce risk but still keeps them consuming cigarettes. This way the industry may prevent or delay some health-conscious smokers from quitting by providing the low-tar alternative. In an advertisement for True cigarettes, a woman smoker testifies: "Considering all I'd heard, I decided to either quit or smoke True. I smoke True" (Federal Trade Commission 1979).

Third World cigarette consumers are offered no such choice. In many countries there are no health warnings or labels on cigarettes. Such a lack of regulation not only fails to protect and educate the smoker, but offers an opportunity for tobacco companies to sell high nicotine and tar cigarettes with impunity. Chapman contends that, despite the tobacco companies' public position pledging to market similar tar and nicotine level cigarettes in Third World countries as they do in industrial countries, there are "double-standards of marketing practice perpetrated by companies who regularly posture about their 'responsibilities' in the Third World" (1990, 75).

Specific marketing campaigns directed to subsections of the female market are also developed, such as R.J. Reynolds' thwarted attempt to launch the Dakota brand in the United States 1990. As mentioned in Chapter One, the target group (according to leaked marketing documents exposed by American health advocates), consisted of blue-collar women between eighteen and twenty-four years of age. The Dakota package resembled blue denim, designed to appeal to the young woman who spends her time "with her boyfriend doing whatever he is doing"(Women vs. Smoking Network 1990) and whose interests were limited to parties and television.

A detailed analysis of several women's brand marketing strategies carried out in the United States revealed that not all women's brands succeed in producing increased sales (Jones 1987). Katherine Jones identified Virginia Slims and More as successful primarily because they stress "independence, glamour, and excitement," as opposed to "femininity, indulgence, or simply a 'pretty'" image (1987, 26). As Ellen Gritz notes, issues for adolescents include developing self-esteem, a self-concept and autonomy (1984, 107), and the images presented to young girls in the successful cigarette ads are those which reflect and inspire such development.

Product design for women has been very carefully planned by the tobacco industry in Europe as well. The Bureau for Action on Smoking Prevention (BASP) in Europe notes:

> According to the tobacco industry, 'the appeal lies in the image of confident, sophisticated, feminine luxury'. Thus, female cigarettes have style, brand names appealing to women (Kim, Capri, Vogue),[3] a longer length (slimness and style), a lower tar content (health concerns), and are packaged and promoted in such a way as to appeal to women (beautiful packets, luxury inner foils, satin like filters, etc). These cigarettes are so feminine that they are universally identified as "female" cigarettes, and smoked only by women. (Karaoglou and Naett 1991, 3)

Many other products and promotional items have been launched to support the introduction of women's brands. These include purses, lighters, diaries, shirts, cigarette cases, makeup, sports clothes, nylon stockings and sunglasses, among other items. Some of these related marketing efforts have been far–fetched, such as the 1930 Lucky Strike campaign to get women to like the colour green, which was their package colour. They even tried to get the fashion industry to link the wearing of green to the most fashionable people.

> One of the well-publicized events in this campaign was a Green Fashion Luncheon with a menu that featured greenbeans, asparagus salad, pistachio mousse glace, and creme de menthe . . . American Tobacco supported symposia of psychologists to discuss the implications of the colour green in the area of mental health. . . . Artists gathered to discuss the use of green in the works of the great masters and found that they approved heartily of the use of the colour. (White 1988, 126)

Promotions and sponsorships of sports, arts and cultural events constitute another significant area of the tobacco industry's market development strategies. Such sponsorships have been banned in Australia but most countries are exposed to this method of gaining visibility even when tobacco advertising bans prevent the products from being promoted. In most Third World countries, arts and sport sponsorships, related promotions and product lines are very common and are serving to accelerate the development of the tobacco market across the world. The amount of such promotion and advertising in the Third World is not a matter of public record, but tobacco brand advertising budgets are some of the largest of any product in countries such as Malaysia, Hong Kong, Kenya, Indonesia and Southern China (Chapman 1990, 76-77).

Much promotion is directed at teens and children as they constitute the most lucrative market for tobacco companies. The marketing methods range from free giveaways to sponsoring teen events. The Salem cigarette company sponsored televised concerts featuring Madonna in Hong Kong and Paula Abdul in Seoul. Teenagers in Budapest are given free Marlboros at rock concerts. Those who accept a light also receive Marlboro sunglasses (Ecenbarger 1993). Teenagers have been directly targeted by Charms campaigns in India and Nojorono in Java, among others. The Charms campaign was based on promoting the lifestyle of the West, labelled the "denim culture" by a commentator in Business India, a trade magazine (Chapman 1990, 77)

While Virginia Slims' promotion of women's tennis in the US and Kim's promotion involving tennis star Martina Navratilova in the UK are the most famous examples, most women's sports and several cultural activities, such as opera, ballet and the exhibition of art, have also traditionally been well supported by tobacco companies. Such support can include the hiring of prominent spokespersons or the naming of events or buildings after the company. Chapman suggests that this form of "indirect advertising" may also include the bribing of television camera people to linger on the logos and signs of the sponsoring company while filming an event (1986, 46).

Sponsorship not only creates advertising venues but, more importantly, it cultivates the dependence and loyalty of sports and arts organizations—an important factor given the current challenges to tobacco advertising in most industrial countries. Even where there are not yet advertising bans, companies already appear to be shifting the focus of their spending from direct advertising to sponsorships (Robinson et al. 1992, S25). The opposition expressed by many of these organizations to bans on sponsorship and promotion has been predictably based on the difficulty of finding alternate sources of financial support. Only in a few jurisdictions (such as Victoria, Australia) has this question been systematically and successfully addressed through creating tax supported foundations designed to replace sponsorship grants.

On a more symbolic level, the tobacco industry's sponsorship of sports has merged the ideas of fitness, health, vigour and athleticism with smoking and cigarettes. The sponsorship of arts and cultural activities impresses the public with ideas of sophistication, glamour and class. Each effort puts tobacco and cigarettes in a more positive light and the ability to sponsor sport symbolically rebuts the widespread health concerns about smoking.

Less visible sponsorship is undertaken in countries around the globe. This often involves underwriting specific organizations, thereby buying their silence or public support on the issue of smoking. Examples of this in the US include industry support to organizations for women, African Americans and Latinos. It is estimated that such groups received over $4.5 million in 1987 alone (ibid.). African American cultural, arts, journalism, business and publishing groups are particularly targeted. Among women's groups, those focused on politics, such as the National Women's Political Caucus and the National Organization for Women are supported by the industry (ibid.; Shear 1985, 6). Because the support to these groups was offered when no other funding was forthcoming, loyalty and affinity has built toward the sponsoring company. Martina Navratilova defends the tobacco sponsorship of women's tennis:

> I think the sponsor has been there a long, long time. I'm thankful they were there when no one else wanted women's tennis, when no one came to watch, no one cared. (Quoted in Robinson et al. 1992, S27).

Ethnic and racial segmentation of the tobacco market has also been accomplished by the tobacco industry. In the United States, for example, 90 per cent of all cigarette (and alcohol) billboards are in Black or Latino communities (Kamber 1990, 10). Further, these advertisements constitute the majority of all advertising in these communities. They largely feature White models, a strategy designed to imply that smoking is a glamorous, upwardly mobile activity. Young African American men and women smoke less than young Whites in the US (Robinson et al. 1994). The tobacco industry's focus on segments of the population with less formal education has led to the targeting of Black and Latino neighbourhoods.

In New Zealand tobacco companies are focusing specifically on Maori and Pacific Island people: "Pacific Islanders. In New Zealand we have a brand called just that. If that's not targeting then I'll eat my hat. I wonder who smokes them?" (C., New Zealand smoker, interviewed by Sarah Thomson for "The Herstories Project" 1994).

The strategy of using lifestyle imagery is widespread in Third World countries with a similar emphasis on Caucasian models engaging in high-class leisure activities. In addition, the billboards and other promotional materials are used extensively "as a means of brightening up an otherwise down-at-heel physical environment" (Chapman 1990, 81). Along with overt advertising, tobacco companies "invest" in communities in Third World countries, through donations or support to drought and famine relief (Ethiopia and Sudan), earthquake relief (Mexico and Ecuador) and typhoon relief (Philippines) (Chapman 1990, 75–76). These humanitarian efforts go a long way in building loyalty, state support and name recognition in countries around the world.

Product promotions are often ethnically and racially directed. In 1984, Ligget and Myers identified Dorado and L&M Supers as brands to be marketed specifically to Hispanics (Gardner 1984, 176). By 1988 an additional brand, Rio, had been developed and marketed to the Hispanic market (White 1988, 130). As Tye (1985, 325) points out, the smoking prevalence among Mexican–American women is 70 per cent lower than among Anglo–American women, which indicates a potential for growth in this market. Among African Americans, three brands account for 60 per cent of the market: Kools, Newport and Salem (White 1988, 130). The indirect promotional activities in this community in the United States are extremely widespread, from supplying prize money and grants to inner-city improvement projects and achievement awards, to supporting the publishers of Black newspapers and thereby preventing them from supporting tobacco advertising bans (White 1988, 130).

Gays and lesbians have recently been targeted by the tobacco industry in its advertising. The gay and lesbian communities are deemed to be "brand–loyal," "starved for [advertiser's] attention" and (in the case of gay men) of above average income (Goebel 1994, 65–67). Even more, lesbians and gay men in the United States display higher than average smoking rates (between 30 and 50 per cent smoke).[4]

This targeting is of concern to gay and lesbian activist organizations such as California-based CLASH (Coalition of Lavender Americans on Smoking and Health). The attempts by the tobacco industry to increase the already high addiction rates, through advertising focusing on the themes of liberation and individualism specifically directed to lesbians and gay men, worry lesbian and gay health care activists. A recent series of Virginia Slims ads focusing on lesbians was analysed by Kevin Goebel. His inquiry reveals that a trio of ads, when absorbed as a whole, send a direct message to lesbians (and potentially women contemplating lesbianism) about the sexually exciting and adventurous aspects of smoking (Goebel 1994, 66).

In addition, the fear that the tobacco companies will increase their funding support to gay and lesbian groups and magazines to buy their silence on the health issues is an overriding worry for health care activitists vocal about the long-term influence on the health of lesbians and gay men.

Other focused campaigns reported by Davis (1987, 731) include the specific targeting of the Jewish community, the military and prison inmates in the United States through promotions, contests and advertisements in specialty magazines. The recently reversed ban on tobacco advertising in Canada blocked such focused campaigning since 1989.

Children and teens of both sexes offer the most lucrative market for the tobacco companies to pursue in industrial countries. Men's smoking rates declined in the 1970s, causing the women's and girls' market to be given renewed emphasis. Whether it was correlation or causation, there was increased consumption in the 1970s among teenage girls in industrial countries (Tye 1985, 325).

A prime example of exploiting the child market is the Camel campaign launched in 1988 in the United States which features a cartoon camel (Old Joe). Since the start of this campaign, Camel's share of the (illegal) children's market in the US has increased from .5 per cent to 32.8 per cent, and 94 per cent of high school students recognize the Old Joe character (Di Franza et al. 1991).

In Australia adolescents are much more likely to purchase the heavily advertised brands of cigarettes than are adults (Chapman and Fitzgerald 1982). British children's recognition of advertisements is linked to which company had recently sponsored a sporting event on television (Davis 1987, 730–31). Among American adolescents the brand preferences are directly coincident with the amount of advertising dollars spent on brand promotion (Robinson et al. 1992, 147).

Discount cigarettes are also important to the price-sensitive youth market, as are packaging strategies such as half-packs, singles, ten-packs and free samples. Another marketing strategy that facilitates children's smoking is the availability of vending machines which allow easy access even in countries prohibiting sales to minors.

The duplicity with which the tobacco companies have treated the issue

of children's smoking is remarkable. "Socially responsible" communications designed for young people have been the industry's prime response to any criticism. In response to public concern about Old Joe, for example, R.J. Reynolds attempted to make amends by sponsoring a billboard campaign to ask children if a picture of a boy smoking in a toilet stall "looks cool?" (Advocacy Institute 1991). In the past, the Tobacco Institute has published pamphlets and advertisements exhorting children to consider smoking "an adult custom based on mature and informed judgment" (Gritz 1984, 108). As Chapman points out, such sanctimonious advice is dispensed in tandem with advertising directly focused on youth (1986, 121–22).

Women and girls are viewed by the companies as key consumers of tobacco. It is ironic that the tobacco companies have perfected the notion of woman-focused advertising and promotion while health promotion in industrial nations has taken several decades to understand the place of gender in smoking. Indeed, as we shall see in Chapter 5, there is still resistance among tobacco control and health education advocates to recognizing and understanding the place of gender and woman-specific cessation programs and studies.

WOMEN AS WORKERS

Women work with tobacco and cigarettes in many ways; they work as retailers, factory workers, growers and promoters. In addition, many of those involved in preventing smoking or dealing with its effects are in female dominated professions and jobs. Despite this, there are very few women who have visible leadership positions in the tobacco control movement, either in Canada or internationally.

Women have long been associated with the tobacco industry. European women were paid to create smoking paraphernalia several centuries ago. Records exist describing fifteenth century British women as clay pipemakers, a status often accompanied by pipe smoking behaviour and other "male" attributes (Bell 1994).

From the classic "cigarette girl" carrying boxes of cigarettes to sell in cinemas to the modern promotions woman in many Third World countries, retailing has always depended on women. Women often model for tobacco advertisements, stand in kiosks offering free samples or sell clothes with tobacco industry logos.

Growing tobacco also involves many women in an increasing number of countries around the world. As tobacco cultivation diminishes in industrial countries due to declining markets and increased regulation, tobacco companies are introducing tobacco farming to many Third World countries. Women work as planters, pickers, trimmers and curers of tobacco leaves, often in debilitating conditions.

Small tobacco farms are the norm in many Third World tobacco growing countries. Tobacco farming often has harmful impacts on the local environment and the health and safety of tobacco workers. Heavy pesticide requirements are potentially poisonous to the farmers and seriously pollute the land and water systems. The enormous amount of wood required to cure tobacco—where this method is still used—has led to serious deforestation without adequate reforestation in many countries such as Uganda, Zimbabwe and Brazil. Further, the tobacco crop exhausts the soil by depleting it of its natural nutrients and reducing its utility for other crops. In some hilly regions, soil erosion on denuded lands is an additional environmental cost (PANOS Briefing 1994).

Most of the physical work on small tobacco farms in Third World countries is done by women. PANOS, an international development agency based in England, claims that women carry the heaviest burden of tobacco growing. In addition to their regular arduous work of vegetable gardening, marketing and cooking and farming the tobacco crop, they must collect the wood for curing the tobacco (ibid.). As deforestation increases, this can mean going further and further afield to find the wood. As water sources are polluted or disrupted, women must also walk further to get water for household use. In some regions of the West Nile in Uganda, deforestation is so severe that wood must be transported from over seventeen kilometres away (Aliro 1993, 11).

Most of the work in Uganda's tobacco industry is done by women. Women work in the fields with babies on their backs, seeding, transplanting, tending, weeding and harvesting. The men step in to grade and bale the tobacco up for market (Muwanga-Bayego 1994, 21). Indeed, some have noted the inequality: "I realise the inequality of our work, but how do I begin to say he is not doing as much work as I do? That would be threatening, and could earn me a divorce" (Andemire Veronica, quoted in Muwanga-Bayego 1994, 21).

While women in some countries are nominally confined to "light work," such as in the Brazilian tobacco processing industry, this is usually merely justification for being paid less than the men. Women collect leaves, cure them and load them in trucks. The work is heavy and the working conditions are unsafe and unhealthy. Headaches, nausea, dizziness, vomiting and miscarriages result. Many women and girls become addicted to nicotine while working with tobacco leaves (da Costa e Silva, "The Herstories Project" 1994b).

In some areas women are engaged in tobacco growing as part of a family business. Women often have conflicting interests in tobacco growing: they need to sustain the family income but also are concerned about the effects of tobacco use on their children or loved ones. A Kentucky tobacco farmer whose mother had died of lung cancer said: "I've told my husband I'm not going to be involved in growing tobacco anymore. I just can't separate growing it from thinking about who might be smoking and dying from it" (Chasteen, "The Herstories Project" 1994). As tobacco growing in industrial countries declines, some women are working within tobacco growing communities like Kentucky to encourage acceptance of this change. Mixed with health concerns is increasing ethical concern about exporting tobacco.

Women are also key in the factory production of cigarettes; indeed, cigars and tobacco processing has long depended on female labour. In Northern Ireland, for example, a tobacco factory worker described her thirty year career. During this period, she too became addicted to cigarettes, no doubt assisted by the regular issue of free cigarettes by her employer even after she retired (Burnside, "The Herstories Project" 1994).

In Indonesia, fifteen million women are employed by the tobacco industry (Karsono, "The Herstories Project" 1994). They work in plantations, picking and curing leaves and in the factories, making white cigarettes as well as krekel (clove-blended) cigarettes. In the villages, some women sell shredded tobacco and betel leaves. Some women have been displaced through mechanization but, for those who work in tobacco, the jobs are valued.

WOMEN AS CAREGIVERS

Not surprisingly, women's caregiving roles have frequently been a focus of attention in tobacco control efforts. Mothers who smoke have been castigated for setting a bad example for their children, particularly their daughters. Pregnant women who smoke have long been considered unthinking and dangerous. Women who smoke in the presence of their children are now, by some, considered to be "child abusers" and, in some cases, custodial mothers who smoke are being challenged for custody of their children (see pages 123–124).

The ultimate caregiving profession, nursing, has also come under scrutiny for the rates of smoking among its members. Immense attention has been paid by researchers to establishing the rates of smoking among nurses and to attempting to understand these rates in a female-dominated health profession devoted to good health. Compared to other professions, such as teaching and medicine, cross-national surveys in at least twenty-one, mostly industrial, countries indicate that nurses have high rates of smoking (Adriaanse, Van Reek, Zandbelt and Evers 1991). Because nurses are expected to set good examples of healthy behaviour, these rates have been the focus of much attention and many programing efforts in several countries.

This attention has revealed that nursing, a female-dominated profession, is a stressful job often unsupported and underacknowledged. In addition, nurses often begin to smoke in nursing school and continue as part of the occupational subculture. But differences between nurses give the most insight into the profession. Community nurses with more job autonomy smoke less while hospital nurses working within the hierarchical medical model smoke more. As women, nurses also experience stress from dual roles and powerlessness, adding to the reasons for smoking. Much pressure has been placed on the nursing profession to lower the rates of smoking among its members but many personal, professional and social factors coalesce to make nurses' smoking behaviour still quite different from that of the other health professions.

Norma Daykin suggests that the sexual division of the labour force which concentrates women in demanding caregiving jobs explains the association with women's smoking, occupation and stress (1993, 97). In particular, job autonomy, sadly lacking for many nurses, is seen to be crucial for engaging in health- promoting behaviour. Not only do women's caregiving roles deflect women's energy from themselves, they also put women under special scrutiny as role models.

WOMEN AS STATISTICS
The toll of smoking in terms of disease and death for women is dramatic and rising. If any other single disease or behaviour had a similar effect, a ground swell of political and public action would surely ensue. But with smoking, a powerful political economy and an ambivalent cultural history create a very different picture.

Every thirty-five minutes a Canadian woman dies as a result of smoking. At least fifteen thousand of the forty thousand Canadians who die each year of smoking related causes are women. Smoking is the leading cause of premature death in Canadian women (Canadian Council on Smoking and

Health 1989). While this situation is similar in many industrial countries, the toll of smoking has yet to become as evident elsewhere. Over the next fifty to one hundred years, however, it is highly likely that similar patterns of smoking and subsequent death and disease in women will appear in the Third World.

The potential illness and death in store for the world's women is staggering. Roughly one half of all smokers will die early from tobacco's effects, losing on average about twenty years of life expectancy (Peto, Lopez, Boreham, Thun and Heath 1994, A–5, 10). By the year 2000 in the industrial countries alone, ten million women (compared to fifty million men) will have died (ibid., A–8). The death rate for men in these countries is beginning to decline while, because of their later start on smoking, women's death rates are still climbing. It takes about twenty years for mortality from smoking to become evident. In countries and regions where the smoking epidemic is still building such as China, India and Africa, the rate of illness and death due to smoking will not be fully evident until the next century. Currently, there is one death in the world every ten seconds from smoking, but Peto et al. (1994, A–99, 103) estimate that this will rise to one death every three seconds within twenty years, largely because of the spread of smoking to Third World countries.

The effects of smoking cigarettes invade almost every major body system and organ. The list of diseases and conditions attributable or linked to smoking grows each year for both women and men. The three major health effects of smoking are heart disease, cancer and lung disease. Specifically, the effects are heart disease and stroke; lung, throat, mouth, larynx, oesophagus, pancreas, kidney and bladder cancers; and emphysema and chronic bronchitis. (For women, there are added associations between smoking and cervical and breast cancers.)

Some of these risks are heightened through interaction between the chemicals in cigarettes and other substances such as alcohol, drugs, occupational or environmental pollutants and birth control pills. Most of these health effects of smoking are long-term and may not appear in a person until after at least two decades of smoking.

For women, there are additional effects. Recent research has revealed links with cervical cancer, breast cancer, osteoporosis, menstrual irregularities and menopausal complications. These are in addition to the more established risks for pregnant women and fetal and infant health first recognized in the 1970s: miscarriage, placental irregularities, premature labour and delivery, reduced fetal growth, stillbirth, reduced breast milk and Sudden Infant Death Syndrome. The increased risks of heart attack (two fold) and stroke (thirty fold) with simultaneous cigarettes and contraceptive pill usage have also been noted (Canadian Council on Smoking and Health 1989).

For women who are passive smokers some of the same diseases may develop. Lung and cervical cancers are linked to passive smoking. For women (and children) who live with smokers the risk of developing smoking related diseases is dramatically increased. Historically, this has put women who live with men at greatest risk as men have been the heaviest smokers.

The task of uncovering the full impact of smoking on the female body is far from complete and will require considerably more effort on the part of medical researchers. Inserting a gender-sensitivity into smoking and health research, as well as into prevention, cessation and education, is a slow process.

Although overall smoking rates have been declining over the last two decades in many (but not all) industrial countries, the greatest reductions are in male smoking rates. As female smoking rates are declining much more slowly, there is a rising proportion of female smokers in the population. In Canada, for example, as a consequence, male and female smoking rates are converging.

While male smoking had peaked in Canada by 1965, the smoking rate for women peaked in the early 1970s (Ferrence 1988, 160). During the last two decades the male smoking rate in Canada has declined dramatically from a high of 53 per cent of the male population in 1966 to 32 per cent in 1994. The female smoking rate, however, has only dropped from 32 per cent in 1966 to 29 per cent in 1994 (*Labour Force Surveys, 1966–86* 1986; Health Canada 1994).

Similar patterns exist in other countries. For example, in Australia men's rates declined from 58 per cent to 30 per cent between 1964 and 1989 while women's net decline was only 1 per cent from 28 per cent to 27 per cent over the same period. In the United Kingdom, men's rates declined by 35 per cent (from 68 per cent to 33 per cent) between 1965 and 1988 while women's rates dropped from 44 per cent to 30 per cent in the same period (Chollat-Traquet 1992, 14–15). In some industrial countries, such as Finland for example, women's rates actually increased during this period, contrary to the male trends. In others, such as Japan, Greece and Spain, women's rates are still increasing. In some Eastern European countries, such as Czechoslovakia, Hungary and Poland, urban women's smoking is similar to that in other industrial countries but rural women in countries such as Bulgaria, Romania and the former USSR still smoke at very low rates (Chollat-Traquet 1992, 15). It is clear that there is no unitary pattern to women's smoking rates across the world as various factors, characteristics and locations are involved.

The rates of smoking (and decline in smoking) among women vary by age, education, employment, language and region. The relationship of ethnicity, "race" and sexual orientation to smoking rates has been investigated in the United States but there are no clear Canadian data on these dimensions. Similarly, dis/ability and class may affect smoking rates among women and girls but little is written about these either. More research is needed on these factors and on issues such as experiencing woman abuse in order to understand how various life circumstances affect women's smoking rates.

The rate of smoking among young women (aged fifteen to nineteen) in Canada is now higher than the rate for young men of the same age.[5] But what is more troubling is that the rate of young women's smoking in Canada has actually *risen* in the past five years, contrary to overall trends. In 1994, 29 per cent of women aged fifteen to nineteen smoked compared to 26 per cent of young men (Health Canada 1994). Unless arrested, this will clearly lead to higher smoking rates among women in older age groups in the future.

In several European countries, such as Austria, Norway, Scotland, Sweden, Switzerland and Wales, more young women than young men are smoking (Chollat-Traquet 1992, 17). While male smokers still generally consume more cigarettes than female smokers, the trend toward higher prevalence for young women is troubling as it will establish long-term higher prevalence for women in those countries. Similar patterns are evident in South America where young women, especially urban, educated young women, are smoking more than young men in Chile, Argentina, Venezuela and Peru (Chollat-Traquet 1992, 24–45; da Costa e Silva 1994a, 2).

Women in Canada with higher formal education are less likely to smoke. For women with university educations, smoking rates in 1986 were only 10 per cent compared to high school graduates at 30 per cent (Millar 1988). Like gender, education is a key variable to be taken into account when attempting to understand current trends in Canadian smoking patterns. According to Lamarche (1985), among unemployed women in Canada, 40 per cent are smokers. Women or girls who live with smokers or who have friends who are smokers are much more likely to smoke than those who do not.

The little research that exists on smoking and tobacco use among Native women and girls in Canada reveals extraordinarily high rates of smoking. In the Northwest Territories, for example, 65 per cent of Dene women and almost 80 per cent of Inuit women use tobacco. By way of comparison, non-Native women in the same region have a smoking rate of 39 per cent (Millar 1989). These high rates of smoking are becoming a key concern of aboriginal groups across Canada and the world[6], and self–governed programs are beginning to address them.[7]

What does the future hold? In Canada, overall smoking rates will probably continue to decline but smoking among young women appears to be rising again. The rates between men and women will probably soon converge with a persistent concentration of smoking among women and men on low incomes. It is impossible to predict the range of smoking behaviour by ethnic, racial or aboriginal status, although completed studies of Canadian aboriginal peoples suggest that high female smoking rates will persist.

Women's smoking rates, compared to men's, may continue to decline slowly. While overall decreases in women's smoking have been encouraging, the slower rate of decline may reflect the greater impact on men's behaviour of health promotion and programs and the earlier dramatic evidence of health effects on men. The slower female rate of decline may reflect women's different life experience and attributed meaning to smoking which may make quitting or not starting more difficult, or at least much less attractive.

Whatever the reasons, there is a current problem as male and female rates begin to converge in some industrialized countries. And, because of trends in young women's smoking patterns, the rate of women's smoking may eventually surpass those of men in all age groups.

TIME AND MONEY

Cigarette prices differ all over the world and are usually very low in newer market areas. In some cases, prices also go up and down according to government tobacco taxation policy. For example, cigarettes in some parts of Canada cost a high of $6.00 per pack in 1994 but were reduced to approximately $2.50 early that year. This change reflected a tobacco tax drop legislated in a (largely successful) attempt to end cigarette smuggling between Canada and the United States.

At the high rate, one pack a day smokers spent $2,190 per year and, at the low rate, $912. For a woman making minimum wage or on social assistance, the higher figure represented between 10 and 20 per cent of her annual income.

For one pack-a-day smokers, assuming that one cigarette takes 10 minutes to smoke, approximately 200 minutes a day are spent smoking. Other tasks may be done at the same time but that 200 minutes per day is occupied time and an opportunity for hundreds of reinforcing drags and exhalations as well as twenty lighting and extinguishing rituals.

Women are robbed of much through smoking. Health and life are the obvious costsw but considerable time, money, land, friends, jobs, relatives and energy are also taken from women.

NOTES

1. Alcohol, tobacco and other "immoralities" were also seen as threats to the middle-class family with its rigid gendered division of labour that was so important to capitalism (Levine 1980, 32-33). Later, the same concerns for the family prompted the repeal of Prohibition and a reversal of moralizing attitudes to revive industry (and create consumption) during the Depression.
2. Albright et al. analysed the frequency of tobacco advertisements in youth and women's magazines between 1960 and 1985 in the US, concluding that a significant increase occurred after men's smoking rates began to decline. They also note that, while "fewer women and adolescents are heavy daily smokers,

in comparison to adult men; . . . their initiation rates are much higher, especially for female adolescents. It seems unlikely that the tobacco industry would conduct such an intensive advertising campaign solely for the purpose of stimulating brand switching in these two consumer groups" (1988, 232).

3. Other "female brand" names include: Silva Thins, More, Eve, Satin, Ritz, Max, Virginia Slims and Silk Cut.

4. Little data collection has taken place on smoking among lesbians and gay men. In the United States, several studies have identified rates ranging from 25 to 50 per cent, usually higher for men than women, and in one study, higher among African American lesbians than White or Asian lesbians. See: Bradford et al. 1994; Skinner 1994; and Goebel 1994.

5. This trend is similar in several industrial countries where, as in Canada, young girls' smoking rates are overtaking young boys' rates for the first time. Not all countries in the world have (as yet) experienced the growth of the overall female smoking rate; indeed, male smoking rates are the primary increasing problem in most less industralized countries. However, in some countries, such as New Zealand, France, Australia, United Kingdom, United States, Sweden and Norway, the phenomenon of girls' smoking rates outstripping boys' is already evident (Amos 1990a; Chollat-Traquet 1992).

6. Maori women in New Zealand have smoking rates of 57 per cent and have the highest female lung cancer rates in the world (Coney 1985).

7. One example is the Mino'Ayaawin Project run by the Native Women's Transition Centre in Winnipeg. This health and well-being program is inclusive of smoking, in the context of extremely high rates (80 per cent) of smoking among residents and staff.

CHAPTER FOUR

BENEFITS

HOW SOCIETY BENEFITS FROM WOMEN'S SMOKING

> Smoking offers symbol and solace to women. Is there a theory of
> women's smoking? How do societies benefit? What would happen
> if women did not smoke?

WHAT DOES SMOKING DO FOR WOMEN?

The costs of smoking are the usual focus of concern in tobacco control
and health promotion work. Less has been said about the "benefits."
These may often appear contradictory to the ultimate benefit of not smoking—
good health and longer lives for women. However, a full understanding of
women's smoking must start with an assessment and analysis of the meanings
of smoking for women and the subsequent benefits for societies in which
women smoke.

We still know surprisingly little about the characteristics of smokers.
Quantitative research that is gender-blind has offered little information
about the quality of women's lives and the impact of life experience on
smoking. Qualitative research and analysis of the smoking behaviour of
women or men has been sadly and surprisingly lacking. Feminist researchers
and others following ethnographic traditions have contributed to smoking
research by deriving crucial information from smokers and using it to design
strategies and programs.

Quantitative research traditions have other weaknesses. Limited data
from countries such as the United States, the United Kingdom and South
Africa reveal that Black women, in general, smoke less than White women
(McLellan 1994, 2-3), Women classified as "coloured" in South Africa,
however, exhibit higher rates than both Black and White women. And
indigenous women in several countries, such as Canada, the United States
and New Zealand, have extremely high rates of smoking compared to White
majority women (ibid.). Similarly, little is known about the relationship
between smoking and dis/ability or smoking and sexual orientation. Citing
difficulties in accessing such information, traditional researchers resolve
not to even try filling these gaps. Hilary Graham, a UK researcher, suggests

the invisibility of lesbians, for example, in many nation-wide surveys and census records completely obscures the links between smoking and sexual orientation (1994, 104).

Survey research is also problematic as many people underestimate smoking behaviour when questioned. Given the cultural sanctions that exist against women's and girls' smoking in Canada, these rates are likely underestimates. Hilary Graham suggests that pregnant women and certain ethnic and racial groups of women may be reluctant to report smoking (1994, 103). In nation-wide household surveys, it is widely assumed that accurate reporting by and about young people who smoke is unlikely to be offered to researchers.

There are few longitudinal studies on smokers (Wetterer and von Troschke 1986, 92). These would offer crucial information on how the meaning of smoking may change for individuals over time. Women in this inquiry acknowledge that beginning to smoke holds very different rewards than continuing, and smoking constantly develops different meanings as time goes on and their circumstances change.

Mixing more qualitative research into ongoing studies of smoking is critical. Without asking smokers to describe their own experience and to interpret their own smoking, past and present, there is no solid foundation on which to build. The testimony of women smokers in this inquiry and resulting theorizing increases our understanding of smoking, offers ideas for programing and clearly suggests that improvements in the overall welfare of women and girls will help prevent smoking.

Is there a theory of women's smoking? The women smokers' testimony in this book is a beginning in what needs to be an ongoing process of information gathering and analysis. Additional research attempts may spiral outward from here and fill in the picture for an increasing range of women in different situations and locations.

The meanings of smoking to women form an extensive web of complexity, ambivalence and, sometimes, contradiction. For women, smoking has utility; it defines social lives and images, harnesses emotion and offers solace. Eventually, though, women smokers interpret their smoking in terms of their identity. What does smoking say about them? What can they possibly say about their smoking?

First, we must place women's voices in context. Women still live in patriarchies, experiencing inequality and power and powerlessness to different degrees. Women often experience inequality in a range of forms: violence, poverty, overwork, discriminations. Women and girls form their identity in such circumstances where norms and power are defined largely by men.

The women smokers' analyses presented in Chapter 2 can be seen as part of the picture and can be used as a starting point for theorizing women's smoking. As bell hooks points out, "any theory that cannot be shared in everyday conversation cannot be used to educate" (1994, 64). The aim of theorizing women's smoking is to develop some insight with women, particularly women smokers, into the behaviour and its meaning. To do this, the themes, subthemes and anecdotes raised in Chapter 2 can be analyzed[1] for dominant messages,[2] overlap and intersection.[3] However, as this inquiry has not tapped women s testimony comprehensively across all groups and regions of the world, it can only begin the process of developing a useful image of women's smoking behaviour. It is hoped that developing theory this way can help transform consciousness, particularly of women smokers. Several of the women quoted in Chapter 2 have informally kept in touch with me to report on the progress of their consciousness regarding smoking. The idea that feminist theory is useful among individual women or groups of women smokers is a reality. As bell hooks reflects on the use of her theorizing among men in prison, it "is not a naive fantasy" that feminist theory can speak to diverse audiences (1994, 72).

Theory-building regarding the meaning of smoking to women needs further development and testing among women of different ages, races, social classes, sexual orientation, abilities and in different countries. Such testing can refine theory and build new theory. It is critical to begin to deal specifically with these factors (such as gender, "race," class, age, dis/ability and sexual orientation) if we are to make progress in theory, policy and program development.

It is to be expected that factors such as gender, "race" and class deeply affect both the experience of being targeted and exploited by the tobacco industry as well as that of being a smoker. While this inquiry has focused on both of these aspects, the testimony about the latter is the basis for theorizing women's smoking in this study. It remains to be seen how theory-building on women's smoking will develop once the differences between women smokers of different identities and locations are more clearly established. To facilitate this process, it is the responsibility of feminist researchers to make accessible to women, particularly women smokers, the thinking and theorizing on women's smoking. Only in this way will truly meaningful and revolutionary understanding and action on this issue occur. Then the following process will undoubtedly occur to the benefit of all concerned with women and smoking:

> If one person's theorizing is sound and correct enough to be useful to another, the other still has to make use of her own knowledge to transpose and interpret it, to adapt it to the details of her own life and circumstances, to make it her own. (Frye 1983, xiv)

If a theory proves useful across social classes within the same country, particularly in countries with a high or waning female smoking rate, it will show that women smokers derive meaning from smoking in similar ways even if material circumstances differ. In the same way, if a theory proves useful across ages, then it will show that the general meanings of smoking for women can be established and derived at any age. I anticipate also that, given preliminary findings, additional studies by race, ability and sexual orientation will be particularly illuminating. It appears that attitudes of racism, ableism and heterosexism have caused these factors to be virtually ignored in anti-smoking research and programing even in the industrial countries.

Issues of identity dominate the analyses of smoking offered by the women in this study. All of the themes lead the women eventually to view smoking as a reflection of many and varied aspects of their identities; in relation to their smoking, they see themselves as deviant, conformist, calm, relaxed, creative, controlled, comforted, guilty, tense, competent, independent, self-protective, social, weak or sophisticated. The problems and contradictions created by smoking are raised by all groups of women included in the study. An intense, internalized contradiction often emerges when these women talk about how their smoking makes sense to them.

While smoking appears to offer great solace and sometimes intense comfort to these women, they have less need to discuss dependency issues. However, the drama of their descriptions of dependency cannot be overlooked, for this is central to re-forming a non-smoking identity.

The women in this study use smoking to *control* both external forces in their lives as well their emotional responses to them. Similarly, they describe how smoking helps them to *adapt* to both their own circumstances as well as to imposed roles. These threads of control and adaptation run through all the voices included here and broaden our understanding of how smoking relates to power and control as they are played out through the lives of women.

WOMEN, SMOKING AND IDENTITY

The need for control and adaptation so apparent in the women's voices reflects two sides of the same prism of responses to being female. Across the globe, women generally continue to have less power than most men in their society in defining social reality. Women end up deriving the meaning of femaleness from systems and values not of their making but manifested in society's institutions such as, in the industrial world, family, church, state, school and the media.

Consequently, definitions of woman remain powered by a male controlled social reality. Although women constantly interact with their communities, thereby generating some of the definition of self and of "woman," the major sources of definition of the female self have come from the public sphere from which women traditionally have been, and in many countries still are, excluded.

That women have agency in these processes is obvious. Women in even the most oppressive circumstances resist, regroup and persevere. However, when definitions of woman are consistently created externally, then buffers, mediators and screens separate inner emotions from the outer life.

Women smokers experience first hand the inconsistency between the female script and their own reality. Women often feel betrayed by the very script that they absorbed on discovering that it contains images of femaleness that do not materialize. This underlies many of the tensions and contradictions described by women when asked to consider the meaning of smoking to them.

Uta Enders-Dragaesser terms this division a "paradoxical social reality" which feels like both a contradiction and a burden (1988, 585). Further, she says:

> dealing with these paradoxes uses up a lot of energy which is then unavailable for other things. This is particularly true for experiences of abuse and violence which we now know occur frequently and often leave traumata which last a lifetime. (ibid., 587)

Consequently, women must spend considerable energy and time "getting used to it," "toeing the line," "playing along" or being a "good sport" in face of the stark reality of inequality (ibid., 585–87). I suggest that smoking is an aid in this process.

At times, this contradiction is lived out through the female body in its deportment, accessorizing and presentation. Assessing women's smoking from this point of view involves exploring the role of smoking from the "inside" of the body as well as the outside. But the definition of women's smoking is constantly being redefined over time and between places. As we saw in Chapter 1, women's smoking has, over several decades, gone from immoral to glamorous to liberated to unhealthy to stupid and marginalized, just in North America! It is not surprising, then, that identity issues are so central and troublesome for women smokers. Women's self-definitions in relation to smoking and the meaning of smoking with respect to women's selves are continually pushed to change.

The meaning(s) of smoking for women from both internal and external sources are multi-layered and variable. In developing a theory of women's smoking, therefore, the interaction between inner and outer life must be acknowledged.

It is useful to apply Sandra Bartky's concept of "disciplinary practices" to women's smoking behaviour. She suggests that there are three practices carried out on women to create femininity and the female identity. These are:

> those that aim to produce a body of a certain size and general

105

configuration; those that bring forth from this body a specific repertoire of gestures, postures, and movements; and those that are directed toward the display of this body as an ornamented surface. (1988, 64)

Aspects of these practices that encourage certain kinds of deportment or emotional style in women are linked to the themes women smokers discuss. For example, Bartky suggests that expressions of women's true emotional states are actively discouraged. Such measures as "wearing a fixed smile" despite one's inner state or eliminating facial wrinkles despite their indication of past emotional experiences are two examples of this type of "disciplinary practice." The use of smoking to suppress negative emotions is another. Such a use of smoking by women can also be seen as a *benefit* to society; if women actually gave vent to the emotions suppressed by smoking, those around them would be forced to react.

While smoking is eventually disempowering, in the meantime it is useful for women in solidifying identity and enhancing power. From this point of view, quitting is not simply a difficult process but becomes a serious loss of part of the equipment of being female.

While women may describe smoking as a burden, it is also a key part of a woman's repertoire. Looked at this way, women demonstrate agency through smoking and, as clearly expressed, would suffer a void in their identity and ability to negotiate social life if they were to give it up. Quitting smoking, then, would constitute what Bartky calls "de-skilling" (1988, 77). Recognizing this consequence is essential to understanding the possibility (or possible limitation) of a non-smoking identity.

Rapidly changing definitions of smoking and increasing regulation of public smoking contribute to contradictions and confusion around the meaning of smoking. These external shifts add to the turmoil of understanding the self in relation to smoking, or smoking in relation to self, by continually changing the rules. So for women, the questions "What does smoking say about me?" and "What can I say about my smoking?" may never be answered conclusively.

The material roots of femininity are also important to understanding the testimony of the women smokers. Dorothy Smith sees the media as key transmitters of the practices, activities and products crucial to being female (1988, 37). Women actively engage with this process as creative players and consumers. Reading women's magazines and buying fashions and cosmetics are examples of this process.

Women use smoking to organize social relationships or to create and project images. These "disciplinary practices" are quite specific and, upon reflection, apparent to them. The deliberateness of using smoking to control behaviour or circumstances or to adapt to external influences is clear. Even under the influence of the political economy of tobacco and powerful cultural messages regarding femininity, the agency of women smokers is very much apparent.

Defining the self in this way can be problematic. If identity is derived from commodities and images provided by the media, attention is deflected "from a more valuable source of identity, namely the historical precedents and the immediate politics of our circumstances" (Finkelstein 1991, 190).

In exactly this sense, smoking functions as a screen between the women and the meaning of their lives. Experience is pushed through a sieve, re-forming reality into a manageable form. Identity develops but is not grounded in pure, clear, unmediated experience. The control and adaptation facilitated by smoking has intervened. Cigarettes offer momentary resolution of the conflicts in women's experiences.

WHAT IS A THEORY OF WOMEN'S SMOKING?
The analysis expressed in the first part of this chapter forms a useful starting point from which to develop a more thorough explanation of women's smoking:

> *Smoking may be an important means through which women control and adapt to both internal and external realities. It mediates between the world of emotions and outside circumstances. It is both a means of reacting to and/or acting upon social reality, and a significant route to self-definition.*

This view reflects the words of the women in this book. A consciousness and self-analysis is revealed by the women smokers, showing awareness of the discrepancies between emotional states and cultural and social expectations. Smoking mediates between these two fields. Women smokers use cigarettes to assist with their taking responsibility for social relationships and the maintenance of emotional equilibrium in their social groups.

Each cigarette serves as a temporary answer to these women's search for meaning. But as each one is stubbed out, the limitations of the answer it provided likely becomes clear. Not only do unpleasant aspects of life re-enter consciousness, but the guilt, contradiction and tension associated with smoking also re-emerge.

Smoking a pack of cigarettes per day may offer repeated "mediations." It protects against full engagement with reality, allowing those realities to continue unabated. This is how smoking benefits the social order surrounding women. Not simply a lucrative and desirable aspect of commerce, fashion or femininity, smoking is also a way of perpetuating unsatisfying and unequal social relations.

The question remains whether women's smoking is a passive or active response to the world. Women can be either "passive victims" of or "active resisters" to patriarchal domination[4] or possibly both, depending on their cultural or subcultural milieu. In some instances, women are victims and are limited to reacting. Other times, we have the energy and opportunity to be proactive in defining the self and negotiating social life. Depending on time, place and personal circumstance, women can use smoking to absorb inequality or resist it.

It is facile to assume that all women are victims. Seen this way, women smokers would be understood to be either completely duped by the culture or driven to smoke as a direct result of their treatment in the world. Neither of these is true. But it is equally facile to assume that a clear sense of self can be forged in a world that largely excludes the female experience in defining female identity. Smoking seems to assist in the assertion of the self in such circumstances.

Women across the social spectrum experience the failure of the ideal, but specific experiences such as abuse help expose the range of ways in which smoking can serve women. These interviews suggest that cigarettes are shock absorbers for abused women; smoking mediates between reality and ideal and eases the rawness of women's pain and life. Not surprisingly, suppressing negative emotions and using cigarettes as comfort were both more common in the testimony of abused women smokers. Many abused women know that directly expressing emotions could be perceived as aggressive and, as such, could potentially further endanger them.

The feminist smokers interviewed consciously analyze their reality. Their conflict centres on the discrepancy between their experience (as feminists and smokers) and their own and others' definitions of feminists and smokers. Is smoking liberating or did they just buy the advertising line? Is their continuing to smoke evidence of disempowerment? Is there a way to analyze this that fits with a feminist critique of the world? Tensions surround the personal and the political and are the source of self-punishment and guilt. The politics of empowerment clash with the fact that these women are being controlled to varying degrees by their need to smoke. But throughout, smoking is useful in negotiating life circumstances.

How *Do* Societies Benefit?

In industrial countries when women use smoking to mediate existence, whether taking the edge off their emotional reactions, giving themselves space and time away from pressures or even staying thin and looking sophisticated, there is often a tangible benefit to others in their society.

Culturally and economically, women's smoking is approved of (in some cultures) in advertising, movies and fashion and as a weight control method. Women's image, size and superficial beauty is treated as a commodity. Generally, when a fashion magazine shows a thin model with a cigarette or a film shows an independent woman defiantly smoking, smoking is seen as positive in the industrial world. Several industries, including the tobacco industry, will benefit directly. Naomi Wolf describes the Western patriarchal definitions of women's beauty and the lucrative industries and practices that support these definitions. She argues that women who smoke to control their weight are actually reflecting the logic of the (North American) culture where women's external body image is valued far more than their internal health. She says women should not be blamed for making the decision to smoke as there is no real social or economic reward for choosing otherwise, nor is there any particular reward for women who live longer (1990, 229–30).

When smoking reduces or erases women's demands, emotions or challenges, women can be seen as compliant and less troublesome. The true scope of women's feelings, particularly anger, remains invisible. Women smokers describe "sucking back anger" with each drag on a cigarette. If women smokers continue to internalize the tensions of interpersonal and social relations, the responsibility of others in their lives to deal with legitimate emotions is lifted.

Some women describe quit attempts that appear to be sabotaged by partners or family members. Sometimes cigarettes will be presented to a woman struggling to quit simply because she is being too irritable or difficult. In fact, this pattern indicates the strength and impact of emotions concealed by smoking.

When women depend on cigarettes instead of a partner or friend in cultures which approve of women's smoking, the pressure and collective responsibility to offer comfort and care is often relieved. The intensity of feelings toward cigarettes as friends and the grief connected to giving them up is a key indicator of some women's security needs that go unfulfilled by others. Both individual and collective responsibility for providing comfort and consistency to women may be abrogated. Recognizing and countering this situation is critical to effective and ethical cessation programing for women. If women are being asked to give up smoking, what can be offered to replace it?

Women smokers are using a socially acceptable (among some cultures) form of self-medication. Unlike alcohol and most other drugs, tobacco does not render a woman incapable of carrying out her more traditional nurturing and caretaking social roles. In fact, as we have seen, it often helps women carry out numerous social roles that are unequal and unsatisfying.

The women in this study generally have few legitimate avenues for expression of negative emotion and angst. While smoking is profoundly self-destructive for a woman, it does not undermine the patriarchal family. Indeed, as long as it does not interfere with child bearing, childrearing and the maintenance of heterosexuality, women's smoking can be regarded as useful by advocates of the status quo to both the woman and her society.

On the other hand, women who get drunk or stoned are unable to care for children or continue working. This is one explanation why women's use of alcohol and drugs is much less acceptable from a Western societal point of view, despite the fact that alcohol consumption and drug use cause much less death and disease than does smoking. Several of the women interviewed, especially the First Nations women, were particularly clear about this. Smoking is most similar to the use of legal drugs—the traditionally overprescribed tranquilizers and sedatives—which have also been used in the service of pacifying women. In this sense, tobacco is a preferred drug, a socially acceptable form of medication.

There are rare exceptions to this. Pregnant women who smoke are the subject of a great deal of attention regarding women and smoking. Indeed, for many years in industrial countries the only form of attention paid to women smokers focused on smoking in pregnancy. Even now, there is an overemphasis on pregnant smokers. Not discounting the serious health problems created by smoking during pregnancy, the best intervention would be respectfully focused on women, not the fetus, long before and long after pregnancy.

A related, more recent concern among anti-smoking activists is the effect of women's smoking on children they are looking after. The issue of children being exposed to smoke, while very important, arouses passions in anti-smoking activists far in excess of the concern invested in women's health. In many instances involving children, societal reaction and attention from the international tobacco control movement has been, and continues to be, swift, sexist and woman-blaming (see Jacobson 1986, 124–26). There is a widespread and strong motivation to intervene in these circumstances.

How can we specify the benefits of women's smoking to a society? As we have seen in Chapter 1, the cultural meaning of women's smoking changes rapidly over time and from place to place. These shifts often affect the development of women's identity and pressure it to fit with new prevailing values and political realities. Over time, this has led to many social meanings being applied to women's smoking. Cultural meanings have demarcated occupations and class groups and evoked images, qualities and aspirations. In contemporary industrialized societies, smoking serves as a socially useful and legal method of self-medication for some women. In Third World countries, or countries where women's smoking rates are low, it may still be a mark of resistance, the emblem of the "bad girl." In either case, smoking is a form of social control.

What would industrial societies do if women did not suppress emotions through smoking? What would happen if women refused to overwork instead of coping through smoking? What would happen if women took control and stopped adapting? Even anti-tobacco activists in the West fail to consider these questions! Could it be that women's health is so undervalued that the benefits to industrial societies of women's smoking will likely be perpetuated and the negative effects of smoking on women will not arouse a great deal of effective concern?

WHY ARE YOUNG WOMEN STILL SMOKING?

As noted earlier, in Canada, since 1990, young women's smoking rates have begun to rise again (Health Canada 1994). Gains made in reducing rates over the previous five years have been reversed. The facts associated with young women's smoking are troubling and puzzling. How can contemporary teenagers (in industrial countries) consider smoking, given what is known about its effects? Further, how can young women appear to resist non-smoking trends even more than young men in modern industrial countries?

While the voices in this inquiry are of adult women, can what we learn from them help us understand why younger women smoke? How might young women use smoking to control and adapt to modern life? When some of the adult women reminisced about their introduction to smoking, there was considerable emphasis on becoming "cool," accepted, adult and rebellious. These aspects of identity formation were salient in their early years. But is adolescent smoking solely an act of rebellion and independence?

The literature on female adolescent identity formation is sparse. Western identity theory traditionally has been based on studies of males, often relatively privileged males. Standard unitary concepts of adolescent identity formation are now being challenged by feminist theorists, among others. The work of Carol Gilligan, Nora Lyons and Trudy Hanmer (1990) attempts to fill this void by offering some ideas about the American private school girls in their study, and the stages of change that adolescence brings.

Their studies suggest that at age eleven, girls are still clear, resistant, strong females. However, Gilligan et al. suggest that the passage between eleven and fifteen results in a diminished, unsure young woman who has seen the culture more clearly and enters a crisis of faith. She learns to keep quiet. These girls, who at age eleven may have been "headstrong" and outgoing, begin to acquiesce to external reality. According to Gilligan, adolescent girls "speak of taking themselves out of relationships as they approach adolescence: about building a little shield, about getting afraid to say you're mad at somebody, about losing track of myself, losing the kind of person I was" (quoted in Robson-Scott 1992, 17). Is it possible that the defences and techniques in building identity, so present for adult women, start so young?

While male (at least, White, privileged male) adolescents are often viewed as on a trajectory of ever-widening opportunities, girls, it seems, face a different reality. Not only are role models fewer for girls generally, but the major influences embodied in social institutions are still male defined. Girls grow to see limits as opposed to possibilities the more they learn through experience. This is the essence of the female paradox in industrial societies. On one hand, a widened potential for girls is presented, but it turns out to be a fiction. As this discrepancy is not usually even made clear, the effect of the illusion is often left for young women to work through on their own.

As Kostash points out, contemporary teenage girls in countries like Canada have been freed of some traditional expectations and limitations concerning their futures. However, the social and economic disadvantages of being a girl (compared to a boy) are apparent early on, and the inextricable cultural pressures to be associated with boys emotionally and sexually are still apparent (1989, 10–11). In addition, working-class, Black, First Nations and disabled adolescent girls, for example, can experience an alienation from the school culture, provoking behaviours that may look a lot like a "culture of resistance" (ibid., 107). Whether this is resistance to femininity, the dominant culture, school or all three, the resistance perpetuates the unequal access to opportunities girls experience.

It is in this context that girls are making decisions that form their identities. When smoking does take root, it does so in this context. Smoking in general is most widespread among the most powerless and marginalized in industrial countries. It appears that teenage girls in these countries are among those who fit this description and adopt the trends of the marginalized. Is the limitation of choice for girls or the dashed relative expectations of choices so severe that girls in Western society increasingly turn to ways of mediating their existence?

Daykin (1993) and Wearing, Wearing and Kelly (1994) have considered girls and smoking in the UK and Australia respectively, contributing to a small but growing effort to develop a sociology of young women and smoking. Both consider the ways in which girls' activities are constrained because of role expectations and sexism both at home and in the community. Girls usually have more domestic responsibilities which constrain their leisure time. Wearing et al. point out that girls are restricted in leisure and sports activities and alienated from both school and occupational systems.

Girls in the industrial world are also exposed to a vast culture of femininity produced by women's magazines and perpetuated in popular films. In magazines, the epitome of mixed messages is sent to young women. On one hand, some rather feminist messages regarding self-development and aspirations are conveyed, but they are planted among a staggering array of articles and advertisements concerning the imperfection of the female body. This contradiction not only affects self image, but also creates the female as a life-long consumer of commodities from makeup to cosmetic surgery to weight loss aids to clothes. Indeed, the female body itself is commodified. In film, the message is more linear. Women are either not present, stereotypically represented or artfully undermined through plot resolutions, character development and theme in popular films. It is rare for a Hollywood film to have a female director and women are given little scope in roles.[5]

Myrna Kostash reflects upon both the higher incidence of smoking and the lower level of physical fitness among teenage girls than teenage boys in Canada. She asks: "Is it possible that girls avoid fitness in some misguided pursuit of female tenderness?" (1989, 85). Kostash also points out the dominance of imagery of femininity in magazines which stresses inactivity for women:

> the woman at leisure, languid upon her chaise longue, gazing into a mirror, absorbed in the passivity of her own useless flesh, her body awaiting the quickening touch of a lover. *This* is femininity. To be lithe and quick, rambunctious and on the move, is to be a kid, a sexless kid. Kids run around whacking balls. *Women* lean back striking poses. (ibid.)

Psychoanalytic theorists have emphasized the emergence of sexual identity during adolescence. Images in media, including those contained in tobacco advertisements and film representations of smoking, feed in to this central identity issue. These images often imply sexuality, sophistication and adult independence. Adolescence is a time of experimentation and of possibility before life-long choices are made. The problem with experimenting with smoking, though, is that life-long addiction may result.

Daykin suggests that the contradictions between the cultural pressures on girls to pursue (hetero)sexual romance and femininity and the independence expected of adults creates stress in young women (1993, 98). She contends that, in times of economic recession, girls and young women have even more difficulty establishing themselves as adults. As adults, the recession has a direct effect on their power base in both the domestic sphere and in the paid work force. Smoking may offer

> symbolic adult status at a time when access to the real thing is undermined both by the paradoxes of femininity, work and adulthood. ... Once established, the smoking habit may be an important means of managing the inherent tensions between and within paid work, domesticity and constraining notions of appropriate sexual identity in young women's lives. (ibid.)

Wearing et al. consider smoking as a leisure activity for girls. In their view, looking at Australia, the school system is a key source of alienation, primarily because it presses girls into a "good girl" stereotype (1994, 634).

Smoking becomes a symbol of active resistance to traditional feminine identity. Because smoking is also useful as a diet aid[6] and is promoted in the popular culture, it can become useful for young women in forming their female identities. This use suggests a passive response to cultural pressures. Either way, tensions grow in adolescent females as they encounter the limits presented by both the domestic sphere and external world. Wearing et al. suggest that "smoking allows women to overcome some of the tension between private self and public identity and so is centralized in their lives" (ibid., 635).

Consequently, girls may be creating their own psychosocial identities through smoking. These initial analyses of young Western women's smoking indicate that a theory of women's smoking based on control and adaptation may also apply to young women and girls. Indeed, such a theory may bear special significance for this group.

CONCLUSION

The time for pursuing individualistic theories of smoking is long past. Focusing on individual weaknesses to explain smoking is becoming less and less popular. However, initial attempts at social and cultural theories to explain women's smoking have also been superficial. For example, the simplistic yet popular association between women's liberation and increases in women's smoking needs to be rejected. The concern about research methodologies capable of capturing the diversity of women's lives has made even the act of theorizing difficult.

Theorizing that women's emancipation in industrial countries has caused women's smoking reflects an overestimation of equality gains for modern women and girls. Only the most uncritical observers parrot this popular tobacco advertising theme. Women and girls in many industrial countries are not experiencing full equality. In fact, it is the discrepancy between what women (and girls) are led to expect and what the reality turns out to be is a key element in why women smoke.

The studies that have been done, including this one, suggest that for the women studied so far—mostly women who are part of the dominant racial group in their society and from the economically developed world—the social and psychological benefits of smoking ameliorate these inequalities. The perpetuation of women's smoking seems assured in the West as long as smoking mediates women's experience in the world and as long as societies need, or continue to accept, all the benefits of women's smoking. In particular, if girls are to be dissuaded from smoking, fundamental changes in the opportunities for girls must occur. Clear shifts in the perception and presentation of the female identity may offer the best antidote to increased smoking among young women. Only through such radical innovations, reflecting an emerging theory of women and smoking, will there be hope of preventing or reversing the current epidemic in industrial countries.

Historically located in those groups with the most disposable income, early trend smoking has typically generated the most "positive" cultural interpretations (portrayed as sophisticated and modern). This has often been promoted in a context of little health education or tobacco control. These factors could have an impact on the development of the meaning of smoking to women. Should all or part of the early trend smoking theory be supported by research in countries where the female smoking rate is still very low, it would show that early trend smoking for women across cultures holds similar meanings.

Testing this theory in countries at earlier stages in the development of women's smoking prevalence and in widely different cultures will also help to understand the global picture of women's smoking. These efforts should be made to see whether the threads of control and adaptation continue to emerge in ongoing investigations.

Japan offers an interesting example. Male smoking rates are very high in Japan but, despite its status as an industrial country, female rates are still quite low (14 per cent; see Chollat-Traquet 1992, 12–14). However, cultural pressures on young Japanese girls may be making them smoke more and more:

> what makes Japanese girls different is that smoking is one of their ways to rebel against the society where women are taught to be obedient, and where for a woman to smoke is considered to be vulgar. . . . It used to be that only bad girls smoked. (Nakano, "The Herstories Project" 1994)

All of the benefits must be understood as we seek to undo or prevent the smoking epidemic among women and girls. Ignoring the psychological benefits or utilities of smoking as women (and girls) perceive them and expecting women to alter their behaviour on the basis of health risk information alone will do little to prevent women's smoking.

Similarly, it is folly to ignore the significant social and economic benefits that societies reap, whatever their stage of economic development. Revealing the real costs and benefits, to societies and to individuals, may change attitudes and raise awareness among girls and women, not simply about the health risks of women's smoking, but also about the considerable social and economic exploitation attached to it.

NOTES

1. The analysis follows the principles of Glaser and Strauss' (1967) ideas of developing "grounded theory." In this sense, the five themes identified in Chapter 3 are categories, and the subthemes discussed are properties or the

elements of the categories. Developing and naming the linkages between these categories forms the basis of the theory. In doing this, the frequency of responses mentioning each theme and subtheme was noted. Using Kirby and McKenna (1989) as a guide, the material was examined for overlap and related properties.

2. The themes that emerged in the Australia–Canada study have been ordered according to the percentage of mentions by the participating women, from greatest to least, as follows:
    1. Identity
    2. Creating an Image
    3. Organizing Social Relationships
    4. Controlling Emotions
    5. Dependency

3. The themes and subthemes overlap and intersect in different ways. Examples of how categories touch each other are illustrated by the following subthemes: 1) bonding and conformity both appear adaptive; 2) distancing and difference can be evidence of controlling external reality; 3) both controllability and independence may reflect smoking as self-governance (control); 4) tensions about identity are often connected to symbol, ritual, independence, difference, support and suppression of negative emotions, some of which reflect adaptation, some control.

4. This concept of victims/resisters is borrowed from: Celermajer 1987.

5. These observations were made in a five part study of film, television, women's magazines, and newspapers consumed in Canada between 1989 and 1994. See Greaves 1995b.

6. While this is pertinent only in cultures where slimness for women is valued, smoking is perceived as useful for weight control. Among some Canadian young women smokers aged eighteen to twenty, 53 per cent of them were worried about their weight compared to only 31 per cent of a comparable group of non-smokers (Feldman, Hodgson and Corber 1985).

CHAPTER FIVE

ACTIONS

PREVENTION, CESSATION, POLICY AND WOMEN

> What has been done to influence women's smoking? What are the effects of tobacco policy on women? What is the role of the women's movement? What can be done to prevent a global epidemic of women's smoking?

SHIFTING THE MEDICAL MEN

Once the domain of the medical establishment, smoking is rapidly becoming more of an issue for politicians, feminists, international development workers, environmentalists, consumer groups, smokers and others. This shift is critical to bringing forward progressive, effective action. The women smokers in this inquiry help to clarify the need to reformulate the issue of smoking.

Bobbie Jacobson's books accelerated the reinterpretation of women's smoking from an exclusively medical problem into one sociopolitical in scope. She began by articulating the invisibility of women's smoking in the medical and health education establishments of several industrial countries (1981). Then, countering the suggestion that women's increasing smoking rates were linked to women's liberation, she highlighted the exploitative tobacco marketing techniques directed at women (1986).

This inquiry is intended to contribute to the goal of setting out actions that may effectively address women's smoking. This idea of purposeful feminist research is stressed by Kirby and McKenna (1989) and by those engaged in participatory action research. One of the goals of this research is to analyze examples of existing policy and programs to illustrate how the knowledge and theory gained by listening to women smokers' testimony may offer some new directions or counsel against some current directions.

The reason that long-term health effects of smoking first became apparent in men in industrial countries was because these men were the first large group to take up cigarette smoking. But this was not initially recognized by the medical community which embraced the idea that lung cancer and cardiovascular disease were "male" diseases. This affected the conceptualization of research and, ultimately, the nature of health promotion campaigns about smoking.

The idea that women smokers may present a different case, medically or behaviourally, was slow to gain acceptance in the medical and health care communities in industrial countries. Following a similar pattern, in Third World countries smoking is still mostly a male practice, thus it may be difficult to raise interest in women's smoking.

The knowledge that smoking is bad for your health is widely understood in many Western countries. I believe it is useful to try to understand the mechanisms through which women, young, Aboriginal and low-income smokers continue to initiate and maintain smoking in the face of this knowledge.

There are many countries where health knowledge regarding smoking is not yet widespread and where basic health care, education or data collection systems do not exist. Even in these circumstances, there are advantages to taking actions on tobacco use from a more holistic point of view. Applying our understanding of the meaning of women's smoking in creating plans for effective early interventions may help prevent the full blossoming of a global women's smoking epidemic.

The International Network of Women Against Tobacco (INWAT) is committed to revising the structure of the tobacco control movement and moving more women into visible leadership positions. While many women are caregivers with smokers and work on program design, few are involved in setting the course for the international tobacco control movement.

In the same way, women and men from the various groups targeted by the industry (by race, class, sexual orientation), and women and men from the Third World, are largely invisible in planning approaches to research, policy and programing to reduce the spread of tobacco. Apart from being discriminatory, these gaps render some of the plans created weak and incomplete. This is a serious problem internationally but, in some specific countries, it is critical.

As the patterns of tobacco consumption shift—from men to women, from industrial countries to Third World, from the powerful to the powerless—wider perspectives are required to effectively deal with all the political, social, psychological and economic issues raised by tobacco use.

WHAT HAS BEEN DONE TO DEAL WITH WOMEN'S SMOKING?

The tobacco industry in North America has aimed its advertising at women since the late 1920s, and its products and marketing campaigns since 1970. Ironically, it is still a struggle in some quarters of the tobacco control movement to validate the emergence of gendered approaches to understanding smoking. Aversion to the redistribution of power and a rejection of feminism combine to prevent some researchers and policymakers from acknowledging the value of a gendered approach.

Some critics claim that, where men's smoking rates are higher than women's, the tobacco control programs created should be focused on men. Others simply see a gendered approach as evidence of feminist redefinition and over-dramatization of a simple problem, that being addiction to a substance through habituated use and the need for more effective general cessation strategies. These critics often overlook the impact of either inequalities or gender on health. They are likely daunted by the scope and immensity of the required solutions to women's smoking that follow from a gendered inequality analysis. Some researchers are reluctant to credit or explore the subjective experiences and analyses of smokers because, as we have seen in this inquiry, the material that emerges can complicate policymaking. When faced with individuals' stories, it becomes especially challenging to enact macro tobacco-control measures that regulate and legislate smoking.

Such resistance is hardly surprising. Redefining smoking as a social problem requires the involvement of different experts, including smokers. It also inspires different strategies in policy, research, program and politics. Bringing this generalized social definition to the problem of women's smoking challenges the authority and influence of traditional expertise.

It is important to see women's smoking behaviour as a societal issue and more than an individual issue. It is too easy to think of women smokers as simply agents of their own poor health or instruments of their own addiction. But a substantial number of members of the tobacco control movement continue to use this sexist and disrespectful approach to inform policy and programing efforts.

When the issue of women and smoking has been considered in the past, the focus has been primarily on either pregnancy or external beauty. The less visible health effects of women's smoking have only begun to be researched in the past few years. Research on the entire spectrum of smoking and women's reproductive health, menopause and cervical and breast cancer is very recent. Even the dramatic risk of cancer posed by combining oral contraceptive use and smoking was researched only after patterns of linkage had been well-established.

Health promotion campaigns in industrial countries have been forced to re-evaluate their messages when women's consumption pattern has failed to reduce as quickly and dramatically as men's. The messages, intended to be gender- neutral, have had some positive effects on men's rates but less effect on women's rates. The assumption that smoking is experienced similarly by men and women led to little questioning of generic campaigns or their educational literature.

We need to make all future research on smoking sex-specific and to create tailored prevention and cessation interventions which recognize differences among women. Early trends in some Third World countries should propel even the most entrenched gender-blind researchers and policymakers into specific considerations of female smoking patterns. If the smoking epidemic reaches women in these countries, as it very likely will do, perhaps the mistake of resisting a gendered approach to research on and prevention of smoking can be avoided.

While in some countries the women's smoking epidemic is barely underway, in other countries there is seventy years of history. The meanings of smoking to women must be identified and studied carefully by any tobacco control group or program planner in each specific racial, class and sociocultural context.

WOMAN-SPECIFIC IS NOT ALWAYS WOMAN-POSITIVE

Health campaigns traditionally promoted a generic "stop-smoking" message. In many parts of the world, this is still the pattern. The first woman-specific prevention and cessation campaigns in industrial countries were focused on smoking during pregnancy which, at one point, was seen as virtually the only issue differentiating female and male smokers. Several campaigns on pregnancy emerged in the 1970s when the rates of women's smoking in industrial countries were first seen as significant.

Is it fair to force your baby to smoke cigarettes?

Health Education Authority (reproduced with permission)

Most of the pregnancy related campaigns were guilt-inducing and woman-blaming. Indeed, it remains extremely difficult to try and deal with smoking during pregnancy in a sensitive manner. Jacobson (1981, 71) reveals that a British smoking cessation campaign featuring a nude, pregnant model with dramatic messages about potential fetal damage was made by a small group of men involved in the Health Education Council. When the American Cancer Society launched its 1985 television commercial featuring a fetus inhaling smoke, American feminists were outraged, believing that the campaign was an anti-choice conspiracy (Jacobson 1986, 125).

Worry about a woman compromising the quality of the fetus, her product, is consistent with a long "uterine tradition" of understanding women's bodies and women's health (Matthews 1987, 17). Smoking cessation programs with this perspective regard women's health as important insofar as women are (as Jacobson wryly worded it) "receptacles for future generations." Jacobson astutely noted, however, that such a campaign "ignores most women most of the time" (1986, 125), thereby minimizing its public health impact. She suggests that other factors, notably nutrition, class and race, are actually the most crucial factors in determining fetal and neonatal health (ibid.). Non-medical factors may also be crucial in determining whether pregnant women smokers can quit. Of the pregnant women who quit in the McBride and Pirie study carried out in Canada and the US, many did so before the first prenatal checkup and most before the fourth month (McBride and Pirie 1990, 165). Those less likely to quit are young, poor and have minimal formal education (Stewart and Dunkley 1985).

It is clear that many women (especially in industrial countries) know smoking and pregnancy are a bad mix. Many women, if not able to quit, reduce their smoking. Most pregnant women who quit do so of their own volition. And, finally, relapse patterns indicate that at least 50 per cent of women who quit during pregnancy have already restarted smoking by the time their babies are one month old (McBride and Pirie 1990).

These points raise interesting questions. If most of the pregnant women who quit (in industrial countries) do so without intervention, the advice and programing directed at pregnant women should take a different focus. It makes more sense to focus on *women's* health as opposed to fetal health, and to press those messages long before and long after pregnancy. Indeed, it has been suggested that giving cessation advice to pregnant women is guilt-inducing and should even be avoided (Bryce and Elkin 1984, 2129).

If youth, poverty and limited education affect quitting during pregnancy, these are the types of factors on which to focus. If relapse rates are so high post-partum, then concentrating on fetal health may be the wrong approach. If women are motivated to quit temporarily for a fetus but not for themselves then messages about the value of women's health *for its own sake* apparently have not been effectively transmitted. These are some of the central issues for those taking such an interest in pregnant smokers.

A minor theme in the early campaigns in industrial countries linked smoking with facial wrinkles. Sexism and ageism were combined to stress that smoking made a woman unattractive, wrinkled and prematurely aged. "Faggash Lil," a woman smoker in a British television commercial, was represented as repulsive and sexually unappealing (Jacobson 1986, 124). Other examples include the "Pretty Face" campaign in Western Australia and the American Cancer Society's (1960s, but still reprinted) "Smoking is Very Glamorous" poster.

SMOKING IS VERY GLAMOROUS

THERE'S NOTHING
MIGHTIER THAN THE SWORD

AMERICAN
CANCER
SOCIETY

FOR MORE INFORMATION CALL THE AMERICAN CANCER SOCIETY
TOLL FREE: 1-800-ACS-2345

909, American Cancer Society, Inc.   (One of three "collector's item" posters staged by the American Cancer Society for a smoking campaign in the 1960s.)   69-(25M)-No. 2163-01

The "smoking causes wrinkles" theme stresses women's superficial beauty, ignoring the many serious life-threatening diseases developing on the inside. Instead of a natural and acceptable sign of aging, wrinkles are redefined as unacceptable and repulsive. Female external beauty is idealized as both eternally youthful and more important than women's internal health. This message is ageist, sexist and unacceptable. Such campaigns could do more harm than good. Reinforcing the primacy of appearance over health in the name of health promotion cannot contribute to healthy body image goals and respect of aging in girls and women. They are consistent with the more recent "beauty culture" formulation of Western attitudes to women's health and bodies described by Matthews (1987, 24–31). These campaigns also serve as a strange echo of Lucy Page Gaston's campaign against "cigarette face" in the early 1900s. She had no health research to bolster her campaign against smoking but maintained that furfural, a chemical in cigarettes, caused this malady which led to drinking, further disease and crime (Sobel 1978, 53).

These two themes reflect a patriarchy fundamentally unconcerned with women's health. Both concentrate on the value of women as externally defined. They epitomize the thrust of the woman-specific smoking prevention and cessation programs in industrial countries in the 1970s and early 1980s. Only after repeated feminist critique, exposing the sexism, ageism and objectification of women, were there any serious efforts to make the value of women and women's health, *for its own sake*, central to women's smoke cessation and prevention.

WOMAN-POSITIVE PREVENTION AND CESSATION PROGRAMS

In 1983, at the Fifth World Conference on Tobacco and Health, the international tobacco control movement decided to identify women as a group for "special concern." Following this, some industrial countries began to consider women a special group requiring tailored tobacco prevention and cessation campaigns.

The resulting efforts in several countries showed improvement by the late 1980s but clearly suffered from a lack of a coherent analysis or theory of women's smoking. Consequently, some campaigns were effectively woman-positive while others in the same country or state were not. There was growing concern about some women's health issues such as oral contraceptive use and smoking the slowly increasing lung cancer rate. Sometimes it was not the theme taken up in the campaigns that caused concern but the approach. Anti-smoking messages were still often couched in a sexist, victim-blaming framework.

Dramatic attempts to engage women tended to backfire, such as suggestions that smoking was dumb, silly or unattractive. These kinds of messages, not surprisingly, were ultimately alienating. Outright sexism also continued; one American prevention poster features a scantily clad woman in a provocative pose with a cigarette in her mouth. The caption reads, "An ugly butt can ruin a great body."

The advertising firms hired to create campaigns proved to be an

additional obstacle. Enlightened health promotion workers found themselves arguing with media experts about effective advertising themes and struggling to create woman-positive campaigns. However, on the basis of more coherent frameworks for woman-positive prevention and cessation themes resulting from increased activism and research on women's smoking, there has been some improvement in the materials produced for women. This growing clarity will hopefully prevent future blunders.

The challenge to create woman-specific and woman-positive prevention and cessation programs has only recently been taken up in a few countries. In Canada, the "Take Control" campaign by the Canadian Council on Smoking and Health, underpinned by a theme of empowering women, was one of the first woman-positive campaigns. In Australia, the "Smoking, Who Needs It?" campaign emerged from research for the National Campaign against drug abuse and was directed at smoking prevention and cessation among young women. While still not common, the development of woman-positive prevention and cessation is spreading in other industrial countries such as the United Kingdom and the United States. In most Third World countries, however, such attention is rare as health workers concentrate on providing basic health information and education about smoking.

Several programs investigating woman-centred approaches to cessation and prevention have been developed in Canada over the past few years. Although consistently under-evaluated, these still represent the best opportunities for discovering the routes to effective woman-positive interventions. Many approaches have been tried, ranging from group sessions to self-help journals to videos and self-help groups for smokers. They have been directed at girls and women, on low-incomes, pregnant teens, Native teens, functionally illiterate women, and nurses, among others.

These initiatives are only a beginning. They raise questions about the best methods of transmitting ideas to women about smoking. Group sessions are costly and reach only a small proportion of smokers. Most smokers report quitting "on their own," so diverse sources of information about smoking are extremely important. Mass media campaigns may reach a lot of people but are hard to tailor to the needs of specific groups. Some women find both of these approaches inaccessible because of language, economics, location or other characteristics. These initiatives have also helped identify women who need more focused attention, such as women in prisons and psychiatric hospitals, women using social services, Native women, Black women, older women, survivors of violence and lesbians.

These efforts point to a reassessment of evaluation criteria. What constitutes success for a woman-centred intervention, whatever its form? Is cessation the only goal? Is reduction of smoking a success? Even if there is a relapse, is that a success? If the prevention or cessation initiative simply raises awareness or persuades smokers, and others, to think about the issues involved, is that enough to support continuing? Some excellent community development work has been inspired by these initiatives and some creative products have resulted from community actions around women's smoking. A video produced by pregnant Native teenagers in Regina has become a popular resource in hundreds of reserves. A kit developed with low-literacy francophone women in Montreal stands out as a fine example of an innovative educational tool. While neither of these programs showed high cessation rates, their influence on the communities is immeasurable.

This inquiry establishes that the issues surrounding smoking and women's identity are complex. This may mean that the path to cessation is long and winding and may hinge on encouraging self-analysis by women smokers of the place of smoking in their lives. The paths to prevention are more difficult to discern but may also benefit directly from more research with young women and girls, both smokers and non-smokers, who could offer some effective insights on considering the place of smoking in their lives.

What Could Programing for Women look like?
Despite recent advances, there is still no widely shared theoretical basis for future woman-specific and woman-positive program development. Based on the women in this inquiry and knowledge from the woman-focused initiatives already underway, some recommendations can be made.

Whether smoking is active rebellion and resistance, passive capitulation to patriarchal reality or a bit of both, it is a statement on a woman's interactive relationship with her sociocultural milieu. Therefore, at root, useful approaches must focus on this relationship. Tobacco prevention and cessation initiatives should be comprehensive and holistic—this need has been recognized repeatedly by women smokers. As we have seen, when women are asked to consider smoking, many related issues emerge.

Each of the five themes in this study reveals different modes of controlling and adapting to life circumstances. Using smoking to mediate the "paradox" of being female in a patriarchal world is legal, logical and beneficial to the social order and the status quo.

Acknowledgment of the importance of women's subjective analyses of smoking must play a part in initiatives, whatever the format. The issues, meanings and uses of smoking in forging identity and negotiating life must form a key part of the actions.

It is also important to define the benefits of women's smoking for those around them and society at large. This knowledge could be empowering as women may find that their smoking serves others, perhaps in ways they would rather change, acknowledge or discourage.

Similarly, the impact of social pressure on the development of women's image and the promotion of smoking as a positive adjunct to this image (through fashion magazines, movies and cigarette ads) can be exposed and included in programing. This would address, from an external location, the use of smoking by women to create and project an image.

Serious prevention and treatment programs must address alternatives. What is our collective responsibility to replace smoking, especially for those strongly connected and dependent upon smoking as symbol and solace? If such community accountability was taken seriously, anti-tobacco activists interested in ending women's smoking would turn some of their attention to wider women's issues.

Those who create and promote such programs must learn from women smokers. All too often, anti-smoking initiatives ignore the expertise and agency of smokers and apply programs in a colonialist manner. The paternalism implied when participants are deemed to be in need of the program planners' message needs to be replaced with a balance of power and respect. Nowhere is this more important than with Aboriginal smokers in many countries. Strong memories of colonization and its damage can best be replaced by not only valuing the input of the participants, but funding, supporting and facilitating self-governed solutions.

Among Canadian Aboriginal people, Native communities are beginning to create their own interventions. These are usually community-based, holistic and initiated by women, although they are often inclusive of both men and women. Examples include the Mino'Ayaawin Project in Winnipeg, co-ordinated by Celeste McKay, and the Pauktuutit National Inuit Tobacco Campaign, both conceived and run by women's organizations.

In these programs, it is important to address and differentiate cigarette smoking from traditional forms of tobacco use. There can be resistance to this because of the special role that tobacco has played in Native communities long before colonization by the Europeans. Also, in Canada, more recent conflicts surrounding the tobacco tax and smuggling issues have been focused on Native communities, particularly those close to the Canadian-American border, where Native reserves have an open-border and tax-free status. These events sometimes solidify the resistance of Natives to conceptualizing smoking as a key issue which is undermining the health of communities. Lucille Bruce, a Native women's advocate for increased tobacco awareness, suggests that both factors contribute to the "denial" surrounding smoking among Native communities (Personal communication 1995).

It goes without saying that initiatives must drop revictimization, blame and devaluation of women and girls. Anything less will impair the development of strong female identities and possibly do more harm than good. Only now is the damage wrought by ill-conceived anti-smoking campaigns aimed at pregnant women being slowly overcome and enlightened discussions about sensitive smoking cessation during pregnancy beginning to occur.

More diverse measures of success for women's programing must also be established. Measures beyond cessation, including the legitimate and measurable goals of reduction of consumption, temporary cessation or a heightened self-awareness of ones' smoking, are all worthwhile but rarely noted.

The anti-smoking messages aimed at women can no longer be confined to focusing on internalized responses, behaviour and emotion. Placing an emphasis on the external world and the benefits it accrues from women's smoking is a major and crucial shift. It is in this arena that women, whether smokers or not, are likely to gain essential political and social perspectives, as well as motivation to engage with the issue. This would help to diffuse the responsibility for preventing and stopping women's smoking. In short, women's smoking would be redefined as society's problem.

Women's smoking is not a simple habit open to easy modification. Preventing smoking in young girls may require considerable investment. Innovative means of developing resistance in young women, better equipping them to reject the limits of the Western idealized female existence, will need to be constructed. Smoking is not only determined by social and psychological factors, but also presents benefits and performs functions for both individual women and the societies in which they exist. Continuing to deny this complexity will ensure ineffective and wasteful programing.

HOW DO TOBACCO POLICIES AFFECT WOMEN?

Tobacco policy also affects women. Policies include laws and regulations on the availability, promotion, sale and consumption of tobacco as well as on its import, export and taxation. Often the creation of government policy on some aspect of tobacco control can have a huge impact on smoking rates. Especially when children's smoking can be affected, tobacco policy is a popular action. Such actions as bans on sales to minors and on tobacco advertising, the creation of generic packaging and warning labels or increasing the prices of cigarettes are all aimed directly at affecting the consumer.

Policy advocates in the tobacco control movement favour such interventions not simply as a way to reduce smoking, but also as a way to battle the tobacco industry. If the suppliers of tobacco can be slowed or halted, then the global war against tobacco may one day be won. Such advocacy can be highly innovative. Using the courts to establish liability for tobacco's damages to smokers or for the costs to state health care funds are two such actions. Forcing disclosure of the ingredients of cigarettes or attempting to have tobacco classified as a hazardous substance to allow tighter control are further examples of pressure on the industry.

In general, broad policy measures are effective, long-term solutions to the public health problem of smoking. While it is always extremely difficult to measure exact impact, the basic principle of restricting access to cigarettes generally lowers consumption. It is harder to demonstrate the axiom that banning advertising will decrease consumption by removing a key influence on consumers. While there is no doubt that tobacco companies resent and resist such bans—this in itself being a telling point—it is difficult to always correlate consumption and advertising.

For example, in the six years since a tobacco advertising ban came into effect in Canada (January 1989), the rates of young peoples' smoking have risen. Among young women, aged fifteen to nineteen, the rate was 21 per cent in 1990 and 29 per cent in 1994.[1] It is curious that these rates increased in a period of not only an advertising ban, but also the highest tobacco prices in recent history.[2] Even so, the international tobacco control movement is aptly fixed on pushing for such bans as a way to limit the industry's recruitment of new customers through developing cigarettes as cultural symbols in new countries. Overall, it is believed that these bans will have the desired effect.

The perspective of policy advocates is fundamentally different than that of programers and educators. While the latter are concerned with directly reaching smokers and potential smokers in order to influence their decisions, the former are more concerned with creating rules and limits to behaviour that will have an indirect impact on the social and cultural images of smoking behaviour. The issues of women smokers' subjectivity and agency, central to the smokers in this study, are not a chief concern for policy advocates in planning their actions. Indeed, such issues complicate a focused preoccupation with increasing legislation and regulation.

Tobacco taxation policy offers a good example of this clash of interests. Children and women are deemed "price-sensitive" by policy advocates and, therefore, most affected by price increases. This is true, due to having less access to money. Therefore, price increasing is seen as a "woman-positive" policy. Not surprisingly, those who work directly with women smokers will experience this policy differently. For a woman on a low-income, putting up the price of cigarettes creates hardship not only for her but for her children.

This is also true in Third World countries when (most often) men in cash poor families become smokers. Early studies in Bangladesh, for example, show that the families suffer nutritional deficits when this occurs (Madely 1985, 443).

Similarly, in some low-income families in the United Kingdom, mothers report that their food budget, not their cigarette budget, is elastic. Detailed study of spending decisions in poor single mother's families reveal that the highest per capita expenditure on tobacco is among one-adult households with children (ASH 1993). In these families, tobacco spending is inversely related to income. Some poor women in the ASH study do not regard tobacco as "non-essential": "If I was economising, I'd cut down on cigarettes but wouldn't give up. I'd stop eating. . . . Food just isn't that important to me but having a cigarette is the only thing I do just for myself" (Lone mother, quoted in ASH 1993, 29)

> Smoking is at the expense of family nutrition and family health. . . . If people are on income support, there is no way they can afford to be smokers. The first thing you will find that women do is to buy their cigarettes and forget to buy their food. They are not people who are "bad mothers." This is an important point to make. (Grace Burnside, "The Herstories Project" 1994).

Only in this kind of research do the latent consequences of policy emerge in true detail. More questions remain to fill out the precise role of taxation and price increases in food-short families, on women's and children's dietary nutrition and on the use of food banks.

Additional research on poor smokers by Marsh and McKay in the United Kingdom indicates that smoking prevalence rates among poor smokers are not being affected by taxation (1994, 81). They conclude that if *only* the poor smoke, then tobacco taxation would become a policy that actually maintained poverty.

It is not known to what extent male and female smokers make different spending decisions. However, men have higher average incomes. Women with male partners often control the food budget which allows tobacco purchases to be made most easily through reducing expenditures on food.

The impact of substantial tobacco tax increases on the microeconomics of the family has been raised by those who work with smokers and understand first-hand the consequences of such policy. Is their argument against tax increases? No. It is more an argument for policy advocates to not only consider, but investigate, the unintended consequences of such policies and to become accountable for them. How could such policies be ameliorated? Perhaps applying equal energy to the establishment of free cessation supports for low-income smokers would be a fine starting point. Lobbying for the earmarking of such tax monies into health foundations to directly fund such programing, a successful approach in several locations (such as Victoria, Australia), is another worthwhile strategy.

The macroeconomics of tobacco are relatively clear: a few transnational companies make enormous profits from cultivating markets for cigarettes, the major focus of campaigns now being disadvantaged groups around the world. For many analysts, therefore, the overall reduction of consumption and the resulting reduction in mortality and morbidity is enough of a reason to increase tobacco taxation. But for a minority, particularly feminist analysts, the inhumanity of increasing tobacco prices for women and the economically disadvantaged, the majority of whom in the Western world are women, remains fraught with contradictions (see Greaves and Ferrence 1992).[3]

In industrial countries where the smoking epidemic in general is on the decline, members of the lowest socioeconomic groups and those most disadvantaged overall are the most likely to smoke. There will be a growing critique of measures that impact unequally on low-income smokers. Anti-poverty and welfare organizations will play an increasing role in these debates. Women, as consumers (whether they themselves are the smokers in the family or not) typically responsible for family budgets and food purchases, will also want to play more prominent roles in policy-setting.

There is an unfortunate presumption that policy advocates in tobacco control are punitive and hard-hearted (Daykin 1993). I know, from direct communication, this is not so. However, an apparently single-minded pursuit of restrictions, untempered by humane consideration of individuals caught in an addictive vice, do much to undermine this viewpoint.

In response to a recent funding cutback in Canada for tobacco control programing, one policy advocate suggested that restrictive legislation is all that is needed to deal with smoking: "Our primary concern is not for the money. If they took away all our money and replaced it with legislation, we'd be happy" (McKenna, *Globe and Mail,* 4 March 1995).

Daykin contends that "authoritarian and punitive initiatives" result from an overemphasis on corporate interests. This approach is not only too deterministic in her view, but also presumes that smokers are passive victims of tobacco advertisers and promotions (1993, 97). The notion of a purely legislative solution to smoking may make some sense from an outcome point of view but not when dealing with the human beings who are smokers. Indeed, Daykin sees some of the contemporary characterization of poor smokers as a form of pathologizing (ibid.). More revealing, however, is the increasing trend to victimize women smokers using their most vulnerable link, their children.

Using the scientific strength of information on the damages caused by passive smoking, some tobacco control advocates primarily in the US are turning their attention to mothers who smoke in front of their children. Now out of the womb, the child exposed to a mother's smoking is seen as an ongoing victim of "child abuse." Sometimes referred to as child endangerment, this issue is the lightening rod for separating those committed to woman-centred policy from those who are not.

There is usually easy agreement on the goal of trying to separate children from environmental smoke as much as possible. Smoke-free home and smoke-free car campaigns are crucial in this regard. However, some advocates for protecting children have focused their energies on court cases featuring custody disputes.

At the Ninth World Conference on Tobacco and Health in Paris in 1994, the workshop instructing others on how to use the court system to wrench custody of children away from smokers was full. Custodial parents, of course, are usually mothers. Calling smoking in front of children "the most pervasive form of child abuse," the presenter, an American lawyer, recommends pulling out all the stops in framing custodial parents who smoke. Just raising the issue in divorce proceedings may "scare" the smoker. If not, use the child as a witness to gain evidence of her or his mother's smoking. If agreements are reached on not smoking in front of the child, use chemical testing to check. He recommends such lawsuits as an effective way to protect children's health. Indeed, in cases of uncontested custody, he advocates that the parents' smoking status be considered as the deciding factor between two parents.

This strategy reveals little analysis of what custodial disputes are generally about. Contested custody cases can often be a reflection of ongoing strategic and legal harassment by abusive men, not genuine investigations into what is in the best interests of the child. Although this approach is not yet a frequently used tactic in Canada, a recent case in British Columbia demonstrates this weakness. A father challenged his smoking ex-wife for custody, despite his former conviction for abusing her. His challenge and history may indicate he has an ongoing need to exert power and control over her and may have little do with the child's best interests. It is clearly not in the child's best interests to be placed in the custody of a convicted abuser. In a celebrated case in California where a child was removed to a neutral home because the mother could not stop smoking, the man was on probation and had lost custody in a previous battle.

This tactic for gaining custody also suggests a lack of understanding of how women are viewed in the US courts. Images of "good mothers" clash with those of "smoking mothers" who cannot stop smoking for their children. Some American legal observers suggest that women smokers do not live up to the ideal of motherhood that judges would certainly use in family court (Fishman 1994, 210). The tactic has been effective. According to the conference presenter, in twelve American states judges have been convinced that smoking is an appropriate consideration in custodial decisions. As long as custodial parents are mostly women and women's smoking trends progress as they are, this is clearly a women's issue.

Some women working with women smokers in Canada, when confronted with this trend of portraying a smoking mother as a child abuser, see themselves as utterly compromised. They feel unable to continue to work with women smokers in good faith should child endangerment be part of the message they were forced to take forward. Assisting women in understanding how smoking hurts both them and their children, and using mothers' caring for their children as a starting point for eliminating smoke from children's environments, is the way to proceed for those who care about women.

In general, policymaking in tobacco control has largely ignored qualitative information about smoking and smokers. It is likely to become more difficult to separate tobacco policy from such realities as those described in this study. The biggest challenge facing the tobacco control movement as it positions itself for the next century is to mix humanity into its strategy. If it fails to do this it will lose what effectiveness it has, especially with regard to women smokers, and will cause divisions in its ranks.

THE ROLE OF THE WOMEN'S MOVEMENT

Traditional tobacco control agencies in many countries make it a practice to condemn the women's movement's apparent neglect of women's smoking without much investigation into the reasons for this. The movement has been considered at least ignorant of women's smoking issues and, at worst, compromised by its complicity with the tobacco industry. Previous silence on the issue of women's smoking has often been taken by the mainstream tobacco control movement to indicate that an unenlightened women's movement is the main problem in women's smoking.

The reasons for the women's movement's silence have been highlighted in the United States (Shear 1985), internationally (Jacobson 1986) and in Canada (Greaves 1987). The main reasons have been tobacco company support of women's magazines, sports and organizations; a full agenda of social and economic issues and woman-specific health issues; a lack of information about women's smoking; and subscription to the idea that smoking was a "freedom of choice issue." By the mid-eighties, however, the occasional feminist voice pressing for more attention to this issue within the movement was heard. These were to raise collective consciousness and to frame the issue of women's smoking not only as a health issue, but as a political issue worthy of feminist attention.

Marie Shear depicts the lack of interest and action of the mainstream American women's movement in the issue of women's smoking as complicity. She identifies the silencing of anti-tobacco activists and the censoring of information about smoking's effects on women, both in women's magazines and organizations such as the National Organization for Women (NOW). She clearly illustrates the pro-tobacco editorial policies of many women's magazines, including *Ms.*, and their links to cigarette advertising revenues. (*Ms.* gave up all their advertising accounts in 1990.)

Broadside, a Canadian feminist magazine, published a challenge to the movement to radicalize its position on women's smoking and to analyze the global patterns of tobacco growing, selling and consumption using an inequality analysis (Greaves and Buist 1986). Designed to build support within the Canadian feminist movement for taking political action on the issue, this shift was also aimed at replacing the attention focused on the psychology of the individual smoker with attention on the state, capitalist and health care systems' actions on women's smoking. Later, the National Action Committee on the Status of Women, a Canadian national lobby group, contributed its support to the passage of the Tobacco Products Control Act in 1988.

Generally, though, the women's movement has been slow to take up smoking as an issue. Women's health groups and women's groups are overstressed and underfunded in dealing with the whole range of health and welfare issues. Woman-specific health issues, such as reproductive rights, took the full attention of women's health groups in North America in the 1980s.

In North America, there are increasing attempts at co-operation between women's health groups, women's organizations and mainstream tobacco control agencies, but the process is slow (Health and Welfare Canada 1988; Health Canada 1995). Some of the past strategies of the tobacco control movement have cost the support of the women's movement and necessitated the building of trust. Key to making these new alliances work is the level of enthusiasm traditional tobacco control agencies show for women and women's issues, not just for smoking. Such a development will be crucial to collaborative efforts to develop meaningful and holistic programs and policy for women smokers.

The International Network of Women Against Tobacco (INWAT) is evidence of a worldwide feminist concern for the issue of women's smoking. Its ability to bring together people from countries in very different stages of the women's smoking epidemic is crucial to developing effective solutions. The organization was formed in the hope that this kind of coalition would shorten the length of the global epidemic.

INWAT also focuses the energies of those interested in the issues of inequality and smoking. The issues of class, race and minority issues are merged in the feminist analysis of smoking and tobacco control. Other organizations such as INFACT (Infant Feeding Action Coalition), a group originally formed to boycott and resist the sale of infant formula in Third World countries, can link with INWAT for support in its strategy to launch an international boycott of the major tobacco companies. In much the same way as infant formula was marketed in the Third World in the 1970s to widespread global condemnation, tobacco is being pushed today. INFACT and other consumer groups such as the IOCU (the International Organization of Consumers Unions) are key in sparking awareness of important consumer and development issues and insisting on corporate accountability.

Advocates in the United States who monitor the targeting of African Americans, low socioeconomic groups, women and minorities are key links in the spreading action against tobacco. They are concerned with undoing the tobacco companies, financial sponsorship of many US Black organizations and magazines. For example, the Uptown Coalition, focused on stopping the marketing of Uptown cigarettes to African Americans, has been extremely successful. The Pathways to Freedom campaign is a quit program aimed at African Americans (Robinson and Pertschuk 1992, 172). Efforts such as these draw in many minority community organizations in the United States and broaden and democratize the tobacco control movement. There are also regional networks of INWAT that develop strength among women's tobacco control advocates around the world.

CLASH (The Coalition of Lavender Americans on Smoking and Health) is a California-based group focused on preventing advertising and sponsorships from exploiting gays and lesbians. It takes political actions to ensure that the tobacco industry gets the message that gays and lesbians will not welcome their attention. In opposition to a Philip Morris brand launch, CLASH presented its own "Special Queens" campaign, successfully undermining the industry's advertising (Goebel 1994, 66).

Feminists have taken up the issue of smoking, although perhaps not in the ways desired by the tobacco control agencies a decade ago. But it is worth remembering that when anti-cigarette legislation was firmly on the agenda of the feminist movement in North America several decades ago, long before the blossoming of the female smoking epidemic, social and economic exploitation, not the health effects of smoking, were the central concern. I am advocating the reclamation and broadening of that agenda as we approach the twenty-first century and the considerable challenge of reducing and preventing what is now a global women's issue and a clear perpetuation of inequality.

WHAT NEEDS TO BE DONE?

There are lower rates of women smoking in many industrial countries than a generation ago. However, there is already clear evidence of problems with the smoking rates of young women, Aboriginal and low-income women. Once more inclusive and sensitive research is carried out, it is possible that other groups of women may also be found to be at risk. As the patterns of women's smoking in industrial countries relocate according to social position, the rates of women's smoking in Third World countries are simply on the way up.

Women's smoking is a mediator of reality. It is important to ask what is wrong with that reality for so many women and girls that makes smoking beneficial for both them and society. The connections between women's smoking and social, economic and political disadvantage is revealing. Not only does this counter justifications for "blaming the victim," but it clearly externalizes the roots of smoking and places them in everyday reality. This knowledge is key to empowering women smokers. It should also be key to establishing the responsibility of societies for women's smoking. The solution to women's smoking will require nothing less than an improvement in women's lot. Appropriate responses to global smoking patterns as they spread across marginalized groups and Third World countries are needed in the form of commitments to supporting their self-determination efforts.

The limits of the medical and epidemiological perspective are being broken, finally allowing social and cultural perspectives to influence program and policy development globally. Previous neglect of "possible subjective benefits of smoking" traditionally led to the denial of "the existence of an everyday logic which involves factors other than medical criteria" (Wetterer and von Troschke 1986, 79). These kinds of sociological knowledge can only help in determining holistic and permanent solutions to women's smoking.

Creating effective policy in health promotion and prevention requires erasing the sexist and disempowering interpretations of women's smoking once and for all. The seriousness of global female smoking trends must be recognized. Policymakers must acknowledge the importance of women's smoking in managing the female experience and broaden their views and concerns accordingly. They need to become interested in women and women's welfare in order to end women's smoking. The orthodoxy of pursuing macro policy solutions that generally ignore the subtleties of women's lives and the value of *women's perceptions* of their lives and behaviours must be questioned.

> "It hooks you in spite of yourself." She looked rather pensive and sad making this statement. She later added that according to her the society has failed to empower women who could enable them to resist such temptations. (Mira Aghi describing Bandana, a woman in India, in "The Herstories Project" 1994)

This inquiry suggests that if women's lives are improved in some tangible ways, smoking may become less important. Consequently, policies improving the protection and welfare of women would have a latent consequence on improving women's health. Encouraging this widening of policy interests in policymakers who have traditionally focused very narrowly on a medical/ health model of tobacco control is difficult as such matters are usually seen as the province of others.

The demographic transition of smoking reveals a growing correlation between smoking and the powerless, a group which includes many women who define little of the public agenda in many countries. These smoking trends do not resemble the composition of the power structure in the tobacco control movement. Those with the most influence in creating policy (in industrial countries) are increasingly distant from the groups most likely to be smokers and, therefore, are less knowledgeable about their life conditions and experience of smoking. This distance limits the actions that will be conceived, considered and carried out. A subjective understanding of the experience of smoking from a female vantage point is necessary to create an effective, relevant and humane response to women's smoking.

There can be no delay in democratizing and making the tobacco control movement representative. Including smokers in this development is a must. Until recently, there has been little involvement of this kind by women and other marginalized groups. As we have seen, even the blunt and distant policy instrument has the potential to influence the identity formation of smokers. If those groups most likely to figure in increased prevalence rates were included in the discussions, then various latent or adverse consequences of policy design may be reduced.

Inclusiveness of this kind would test ideas for programs and policies at the root. Negative or inaccurate attitudes about smokers, and particular groups of smokers, are more difficult to maintain when face to face involvement is a feature of developing interventions. Sadly, many current tobacco control advocates do not associate with smokers, either by omission or due to disdain. Until these attitudes are acknowledged and examined, policy results will be unsatisfactory, incomplete and lacking in authenticity.

This inquiry indicates that smoking is an important aspect of identity development for women smokers and its subjective meaning multidimensional and complex. The implications of smoking being a way for women to negotiate life circumstances and society's stake in this negotiation are crucial to developing a greater understanding of the global women's smoking epidemic.

The urgency of developing a greater understanding of women's smoking cannot be overstated. The full blossoming of the potential global female smoking epidemic is only now beginning, with alarming projections of massive female morbidity and mortality. The meaning of women's smoking is connected to many other aspects of women's lives. Understanding these connections could inform more effective efforts at prevention and cessation of women's smoking, potentially improving the quality of some women's lives around the world. Is it possible that any of the mistakes and lessons made in the industrial world can be helpful in seeking solutions to women's smoking around the globe? That story will be told in the next century.

The issues connected to women's smoking are many. There is a long history in the Western world of cultural ambivalence regarding women's smoking which is showing no signs of abatement. The tobacco industry's interest in women and girls, as well as other specific groups, is as strong and duplicitous as ever. The spread of tobacco across the Third World's populations is accelerating, despite the concerted actions of progressive groups rushing to reduce its effect.

But the best defence may be in understanding the experiences of individuals. When a woman lights a cigarette, what is represented, what is accomplished, what is helped? This inquiry has shown that smoking can be a screen for women, mediating between reality and emotions. Each cigarette helps a bit in controlling life and adapting to circumstances. To solve this important health problem, then, a global effort to improve the circumstances of the world's girls and women may be the very best first step.

NOTES

1. Health Canada 1994.
2. It was February 1994 when the federal government in Canada reduced the tobacco tax in response to an active cigarette smuggling problem. This lowered the price of a package of cigarettes in some areas of Canada by over half, to roughly $2.50 to $3.00.
3. All sides of this debate are included in the Greaves and Ferrence 1992 article.

REFERENCES

Adriaanse, H., J. Van Reek, L. Zandbelt, G. Evers. "Nurses' Smoking Worldwide. A Review of 73 Surveys on Nurses' Tobacco Consumption in 21 countries in the Period 1959–1988." *International Journal of Nursing Studies*, 28, 4 (1991):361–75.

Advocacy Institute. *Action Alert*, 18, December 1991.

Aghi, M. Case #2, Urban. "The Herstories Project." International Network of Women Against Tobacco, 1994.

Albright, C., D. Altman, M. Slater, N. Maccoby. "Cigarette Advertisements in Magazines: Evidence for a Differential Focus on Women's and Youth Magazines." *Health Education Quarterly*, 15, 2 (Summer 1988):225–33.

Aliro, O. *Paying the Price of Growing Tobacco*. London: The PANOS Institute, 1993.

American Cancer Society. *World Smoking and Health. Herstories*, 19, 2 (1994).

Amos, A. "Women's Magazines and Smoking." *Health Education Journal*, 43, 2/3 (1984):45–50.

_____. "Starting to Smoke: An Overview." Paper presented at the Seventh World Conference on Tobacco or Health, Western Australia, 1990a.

_____. "Women's Magazines and Tobacco—Preliminary Findings of a Survey of the Top Women's Magazines in Europe." In B. Durston and K. Jamrozik (eds.), *The Global War, Proceedings of the Seventh World Conference on Tobacco or Health*. Western Australia: Health Department of Western Australia, 1990b, 912–16.

ASH. *Her Share of Misfortune: An Expert Report of the ASH. Her Share of Misfortune: An Expert Report of the ASH Working Group on Women and Smoking*. London: Action on Smoking and Health, 1993. *Working Group on Women and Smoking*. London: Action on Smoking and Health, 1993.

_____. Working Group on Women and Smoking. *Smoke Still Gets In Her Eyes*. London: Action on Smoking and Health, 1990.

Banner, L. *American Beauty*. New York: Alfred Knopf, 1983.

Bartky, S.L. "Foucault, Femininity, and the Modernization of Patriarchal Power." In I. Diamond and L. Lee Quimby (eds.), *Feminism and Foucault: Reflections on Resistance*. Boston: Northeastern University Press, 1988, 61–86.

Bell, A. "Widows, 'Free Sisters,' and 'Independent Girls': Female Pipemakers in Great Britain 1640–1920." Paper presented at the Society for Historical Archaeology 1994 Conference Symposium, Vancouver, 5–9 January 1994.

Bradford J., C. Ryan and E. Rothblum. "National Lesbian Health Care Survey: Implications for Mental Health Care." *Journal of Consulting and Clinical*

Psychology, 62, 2 (1994):228–42.

Bruce, Lucille. Personal Communication, 1995.

Bryce, R. and M. Elkin, "Lifestyle in Pregnancy." *Canadian Family Physician*, 30 (October 1984):2127–30.

Burnside, G. Northern Ireland 'Her' Story. "The Herstories Project." International Network of Women Against Tobacco, 1994.

The CBC Journal. Toronto: CBC Television, 1 April 1991.

Canadian Council on Smoking and Health. *Taking Control: An Action Handbook on Women and Tobacco*. Ottawa: Canadian Council on Smoking and Health, 1989.

Celermajer, D. "Submission and Rebellion: Anorexia and a Feminism of the Body." *Australian Feminist Studies*, 5 (Summer 1987):57–69.

Chapman, S. *Great Expectorations: Advertising and the Tobacco Industry*. London: Comedia Publishing Group, 1986.

Chapman, S. and B. Fitzgerald. "Brand Preference and Advertising Recall in Adolescent Smokers: Some Implications for Health Promotion." *American Journal of Public Health*, 72, 5 (1982): 491–94.

Chapman, S. with Wong Wai Leng. *Tobacco Control in the Third World: A Resource Atlas*. Penang, Malaysia: International Organization of Consumer Unions, 1990.

Chasteen, C. Tobacco and Kentucky Women. "The Herstories Project." International Network of Women Against Tobacco, 1994.

Chollat-Traquet, C. *Women and Tobacco*. Geneva: World Health Organization, 1992.

Coney, S. "Desperately Seeking Soothing." *New Outlook,* 11/12 (1985).

Connolly, G. Freedom From Aggression. "Resisting Tobacco in Developing Countries." Working papers in support of the Eighth World Conference on Tobacco or Health. Buenos Aires: American Cancer Society, 1992.

Cook, L. and J. Milner. "Smoking Symbols: Gender, Tobacco Use, and the Archaeological Record." Paper presented at the Society for Historical Archaeology annual meetings, Richmond, Virginia, January 1991.

Corti, E. *A History of Smoking*. London: George Harrup, 1931.

da Costa e Silva, V. "Tobacco and Our Earth." Paper presented at the Ninth World Conference on Tobacco and Health, Paris, 1994a.

————. Welcome to Arapiraca. "The Herstories Project." International Network of Women Against Tobacco, 1994b.

Davis, R. "Current Trends in Cigarette Advertising and Marketing." *The New England Journal of Medicine*, 316, 12 (1987):725–32.

Daykin, N. "Young Women and Smoking: Towards a Sociological Account." *Health Promotion International*, 8, 2 (1993):95–102.

Di Franza, J., J. Richard, P. Paulman, N. Wolf-Gillespie, C. Fletcher, R. Jaffe and D. Murray. "RJR Nabisco's Cartoon Camel Promotes Camel Cigarettes To Children." *Journal of the American Medical Association*, 266 (1991):3149–53.

Ecenbarger, W. "America's New Merchants of Death." *Reader's Digest*, Pleasantville, New York. April 1993.

Ehrenreich, B. and D. English. *For Her Own Good: 150 Years of the Experts' Advice to Women*. Anchor Books, 1979.

Elkind, A. "The Social Definition of Women's Smoking Behaviour." *Soc. Sci. Med.,* 20, 12 (1985):1269–78.

Enders-Dragaesser, U. "Women's Identity and Development Within a Paradoxical Reality." *Women's Studies International* Forum, 11, 6 (1988):583–90.

Ernster, V. "Mixed Messages for Women, A Social History of Cigarette Smoking and Advertising." *New York State Journal of Medicine* (July 1985):335–40.

Ewen, S. *Captains of Consciousness: Advertising and the Social Roots of the Consumer Culture.* London: McGraw Hill, 1976.

Federal Trade Commission. *Report to Congress Pursuant to the Public Health Cigarette Smoking Act.* Washington: Federal Trade Commission, December 1979.

Feldman, W., C. Hodgson and S. Corber. "Relationship Between Higher Prevalence of Smoking and Weight Concern Amongst Adolescent Girls." *Canadian Journal of Public Health*, 76 (May/June 1985):204–06.

Ferrence, R. "Sex Differences in Cigarette Smoking in Canada, 1900–1978: A Reconstructed Cohort Study." *Canadian Journal of Public Health*, 79 (May/June 1988):160–65.

Finkelstein, J. *The Fashioned Self.* Philadelphia: Temple University Press, 1991.

Fishman, S. "A Smoker's Tale." *Vogue* (May 1994):200-09.

Frye, M. *The Politics of Reality: Essays in Feminist Theory.* Trumansburg: Crossing Press, 1983.

Garber, M. *Vested Interests: Cross-Dressing and Cultural Anxiety.* London: Routledge, 1992.

Gardner, F. "Smoke With a Spanish Accent?" *Marketing and Media Decisions*, 19 (July 1984):34–37.

Gilligan, C., N. Lyons and T. Hanmer (eds.). *Making Connections.* Cambridge, MA: Harvard University Press, 1990.

Glaser, B.G. and A.L. Strauss. *The Discovery of Grounded Theory: Strategies for Qualitative Research.* Chicago: Aldine Publishing, 1967.

Goebel, K. "Lesbians and Gays Face Tobacco Targeting." *Tobacco Control: An International Journal*, 3, 1 (Spring 1994):65–67.

Gorecka, D. "Tobacco and Our Dreams." Paper presented at the Ninth World Conference on Tobacco and Health, Paris, 1994a.

Graham, H. *When Life's a Drag: Women, Smoking and Disadvantage.* London: Department of Health, 1993.

_____. "Surviving By Smoking." In S. Wilkinson and C. Kitzinger (eds.), *Women and Health: Feminist Perspectives.* London: Taylor and Francis, 1994.

Greaves, L. "History of Canadian Women's Use of Alcohol, Tobacco and Other Drugs." In M. Adrian, M. Eliany and C. Lundy (eds.), *Women's Use of Alcohol and Other Drugs.* Toronto: Addiction Research Foundation, 1995a.

_____. *Mixed Messages: Women, Tobacco and the Media.* Ottawa: Health Canada, 1995b.

_____. *The Meaning of Smoking to Women: Women, Smoking and Identity.* PhD thesis. Australia: Monash University, 1993.

_____. *Update to the Background Paper on Women and Tobacco.* Ottawa: Health and Welfare Canada, 1990a.

_____. "The Prevention and Cessation of Tobacco Use: How Are Women a Special Case?" Paper presented at the Seventh World Conference on Tobacco or Health, Perth, Australia, 1990b.

_____. "The Meaning of Smoking to Women." In B. Durston and K. Jamrozik (eds.), *The Global War: Proceedings of the Seventh World Conference on Tobacco or Health.* Western Australia: Health Department of Western Australia, 1990c, 905–07.

_____. *Taking Control: An Action Handbook on Women and Tobacco.* Ottawa: Canadian Council on Smoking and Health, 1989.

_____. *Background Paper on Women and Tobacco.* Ottawa: Health and Welfare Canada, 1987.

Greaves, L. and M.L. Buist. "The Tobacco Industry: Weeding Women Out." *Broadside*, 7,7 (May 1986):8–10.

Greaves, L. and R. Ferrence. "A Debate on Tobacco Taxation Policy." *Chronic Diseases in Canada*, 13, 4 (July–August 1992):58–60.

Gritz, E. "Cigarette Smoking By Adolescent Females: Implications for Health and Behaviour." *Women and Health*, 9, 2/3 (1984):103–15.

Health Canada. *Women and Tobacco: A Framework for Action.* April 1995. Ottawa.

_____. *Survey on Smoking in Canada*, Cycle 1, #5, Profile of Youth Aged 15-19, August 1994.

Health and Welfare Canada. *National Workshop on Women and Tobacco: Proceedings.* Ottawa: Health and Welfare Canada, 7-9 March 1988.

hooks, b. *Teaching to Transgress.* Routledge: New York, 1994.

_____. *Talking Back.* Boston: South End Press, 1989.

Howe, H. "An Historical Review of Women, Smoking and Advertising." *Health Education* (May/June 1984):3–9.

International Network of Women Against Tobacco. "The Herstories Project." New York: International Network of Women Against Tobacco, 1994.

Jacobson, B. *Beating the Ladykillers.* London: Pluto Press, 1986.

_____. *The Ladykillers: Why Smoking is a Feminist Issue.* London: Pluto Press, 1981.

Jones, K. *Women's Brands: Cigarette Advertising Explicitly Directed Toward Women.* Cambridge: Institute for the Study of Smoking Behavior and Policy, 1987.

Kamber, M. "Signs of Life, Signs of Death." *Z Magazine* (May 1990):9–14.

Karaoglou, A. and C. Naett. *Is She Still A Smoker?* Brussels: European Bureau for Action on Smoking Prevention, 1991.

Karsono, R. Woman and Tobacco in Indonesia. "The Herstories Project." New York: International Network of Women Against Tobacco, 1994.

Kirby, S. and K. McKenna. *Experience, Research, Social Change: Methods from the Margins.* Toronto: Garamond Press, 1989.

Kostash, M. *No Kidding: Inside the World of Teenage Girls.* Toronto: McClelland and Stewart, 1989.

Labour Force Surveys, 1966–86. Ottawa: Health and Welfare Canada, 1986.

Lamarche, P. *Health Promotion Survey: The Use of Tobacco in Canada.* Ottawa: Health and Welfare Canada, 1985.

Lasch, C. *The Culture of Narcissism.* New York: Norton, 1979.

Leiss, W., S. Kline and S. Jhally. *Social Communication in Advertising.* Toronto: Methuen (2nd edition), 1990.

Levine, H. "Temperance and Prohibition in America." In G. Edwards (ed.), *Drug Use and Misuse: Cultural Perspectives.* New York: St. Martins Press, 1983, 187–200.

_____. "Temperance and Women in 19th Century United States." In O. Kalant (ed.), *Alcohol and Drug Problems in Women*. New York: Plenum Press, 1980, 25–67.

Life Magazine. "Clubwomen Get Lessons in Cigarette Smoking." *Life (Fall 1986):*87–88.

Madeley J. "How Smoking Promotes Hunger." *New York State Journal of Medicine*, 85, 7 (July 1985):442–43.

Magnus, P. "Superman and the Marlboro Woman." *New York State Journal of Medicine*, 85, 7 (July 1985):342–43.

Marchand, R. *Advertising the American Dream: Making Way for Modernity 1920–1940*. Berkeley: University of California Press, 1985.

Marsh, A. and S. McKay. *Poor Smokers*. London: Policy Studies Institutes, 1994.

Matthews, J. "Building the Body Beautiful: The Femininity of Modernity." *Australian Feminist Studies*, 5 (Summer 1987):17-34.

McCracken, G. *Got a Smoke?: A Cultural Account of Tobacco in the Lives of Contemporary Teens*. Ontario: Ministry of Health, 1992.

McBride, C. and P. Pirie. "Postpartum Smoking Relapse." *Addictive Behaviours*, 15 (1990):165-68.

McKee, S. *Jubilee History of the Ontario Women's Christian Temperance Union: 1877–1927*. Whitby: George Goodfellow and Son, 1927.

McKenna, B. "Ottawa Slashes Anti-Smoking Campaign." *Globe and Mail* (4 March 1995 A4).

McLellan, D. "Women and Our Diversity." Paper presented at the Ninth World Conference on Tobacco and Health, Paris, 1994a.

Millar, W.J. *Tobacco Use by Youth in the Canadian Arctic*. Ottawa: Health and Welfare Canada, 1989.

_____. *Smoking Behaviour of Canadians: 1986*. Ottawa: Health and Welfare Canada, 1988.

Miller, G. "The 'Less Hazardous' Cigarette: A Deadly Delusion." *New York State Journal of Medicine* (July 1985):313–17.

Mohanty, C. T., Russo, A. and Torres, L. eds. *Third World Women and the Politics of Feminism*. Bloomington: Indiana University Press, 1991.

Muwanga-Bayego, H. "Ceaseless Calendar." *Panoscope*, 41 (October 1994):21.

Nakano, N. "The Herstories Project." International Network of Women Against Tobacco, 1994.

Oakley, A. "Smoking in Pregnancy: Smokescreen or Risk Factor? Towards a Materialist Analysis." *Sociology of Health and Illness*, 11, 4 (1989):311–35.

PANOS Briefing. *Tobacco: The Smoke Blows South*. London: PANOS, 1994:8–9.

Peto, R., A. Lopez, J. Boreham, M. Thun and C. Heath. *Mortality from Smoking in Developed Countries, 1950–2000: Indirect Estimates from National Vital Statistics*. Oxford: Oxford University Press, 1994.

Post, Emily. *Good Housekeeping*. "The Etiquette of Smoking." *Good Housekeeping*, III, 3 (September 1940):37.

Rich, A. "Compulsory Heterosexuality and Lesbian Existence." *Signs: A Journal of Women in Culture and Society*, 5, 4 (1980):631–60.

Robicsek, F. *The Smoking Gods*. Oklahoma City: University of Oklahoma Press, 1978.

Robinson, R., M. Barry, M. Bloch, S. Glantz, J. Jordan, K.B. Murray, E. Popper, C.

Sutton, K. Tarr-Whelan, M. Themba and S. Younger. "Report of the Tobacco Policy Research Group on Marketing and Promotions Targeted at African Americans, Latinos, and Women." *Tobacco Control*, 1(suppl.) (1992):S24–S30.

Robinson R. and M. Pertschuk. "Smoking and African Americans." In S. Samuels and M. Smith (eds.), *Improving the Health of the Poor*. Menlo Park, CA: The Henry J. Kaiser Family Foundation, 1992.

Robinson, R., D. Shelton, R. Merritt, F. Hodge, R. Lew, E. Lopez, P. Toy and D. Yach. "Tobacco Control Strategies: Communities of Color in the United States and The Republic of South Africa." Paper presented at the Ninth World Conference on Tobacco and Health, Paris, 1994.

Robson-Scott, M. "The Growing Pains of Girls." *Buenos Aires Herald* (Sunday 22 March 1992):17.

Rogers, D. "Targeting Women." *Tobacco Reporter* (February 1982):8.

Saturday Evening Post, 7 December 1929.

Sexton, D. and P. Haberman. "Women in Magazine Advertisments." *Journal of Advertising Research*, 14, 4 (August 1974):41–46.

Shear, M. "The Pro-Death Lobby." *The Women's Review of Books* 11, 6 (March 1985):6–8.

Silverstein, B. and L. Kozlowski. "The Availability of Low-Nicotine Cigarettes as a Cause of Cigarette Smoking Among Teenage Females." *Journal of Health and Social Behaviour* 21, (December 1980):383–88.

Skinner, W. "The Prevalence of Demographic Predictors of Illicit and Licit Drug Use among Lesbians and Gay Men." *American Journal of Public Health*, 84, 8 (August 1994):1307–09.

Smith, D. "Femininity as Discourse." In L. Roman and L. Christian-Smith (eds.), *Becoming Feminine: The Politics of Popular Culture*. London: The Falmer Press, 1988, 37–59.

Sobel, R. *They Satisfy: The Cigarette in American Life*. Garden City, NY: Anchor Books, 1978.

Star Weekly, The. "Tobacco Fund Needs Donations Right Now." *The Star Weekly* (25 November 1944).

Stevens P., J. Green and L. Primavera. "Predicting Successful Smoking Cessation." *The Journal of Social Psychology*, 118 (1982):235–41.

Stewart, P. and G. Dunkley. "Smoking and Health Care Patterns Among Pregnant Women." *Canadian Medical Association Journal*, 133 (1985):989–94.

Taxi magazine (January 1990).

Thomson, S. "The Herstories Project." International Network of Women Against Tobacco, 1994.

Columbia School of Social Work. "Reducing Cancer Risks Among Native American Youth in the Northeast." *Tobacco Stories*. New York: Columbia School of Social Work, 1992.

Tolstoi, L. "The Ethics of Wine-Drinking and Tobacco Smoking." *Contemporary Review*, 59 (1891):170–87.

Troyer, R. and G. Markle. *Cigarettes: The Battle Over Smoking*. New Brunswick, NJ: Rutgers University Press, 1983.

Tuya, D.M. Women and Tobacco in Spain. "The Herstories Project." International Network of Women Against Tobacco, 1994.

Tye, J. "Cigarette Marketing: Ethical Conservatism or Corporate Violence?" *New York State Journal of Medicine* (July 1985):324–27.

United States Public Health Service. "The Health Consequences of Smoking For Women." A Report of the Surgeon General, US Department of Health and Human Services, Washington, 1980.

Wearing, B., S. Wearing and K. Kelly. "Adolescent Women, Identity and Smoking: Leisure Experience as Resistance." *Sociology of Health and Illness*, 16, 5 (1994):626–43).

Wetterer, A. and J. von Troschke. *Smoker Motivation*. Berlin: Springer-Verlag, 1986.

White, L. *Merchants of Death: The American Tobacco Industry*. New York: William Morrow, 1988.

Wolf, N. *The Beauty Myth*. London: Vintage, 1990.

Women vs. Smoking Network. "The Dakota Papers." Paper presented at the Seventh World Conference on Tobacco or Health, Western Australia, 1990.